Speak, Lord

Speak, Lord

for Your servant is listening

CAROL ARMSTRONG
BROWN

Pleasant Word
A Division of WINEPRESS PUBLISHING

© 2004 by Carol Brown. All rights reserved.

Printed in the United States of America

Packaged by Pleasant Word, a division of Winepress Publishing, PO Box 428, Enumclaw, WA 98022. The views expressed or implied in this work do not necessarily reflect those of Pleasant Word, a division of Winepress Publishing. Ultimate design, content, and editorial accuracy of this work are the responsibilities of the author.

No part of this publication may be reproduced, stored in a retrieval system, or transmitted in any way by any means—electronic, mechanical, photocopy, recording, or otherwise —without the prior permission of the copyright holder, except as provided by USA copyright law.

Scriptures are taken from the Holy Bible, New International Version, Copyright © 1973, 1978, 1984 by the International Bible Society. Used by permission of Zondervan Publishing House. The "NIV" and "New International Version" trademarks are registered in the United States Patent and Trademark Office by International Bible Society.

Scripture references are taken from the King James Version of the Bible.

Scripture references are taken from the New American Standard Bible, © 1960, 1963, 1968, 1971, 1972, 1973, 1975, 1977 by The Lockman Foundation. Used by permission.

ISBN 1-4141-0089-2
Library of Congress Catalog Card Number: 2003115231

Preface

I came away from a class taught by Sara Trollinger entitled *How to Listen to the Lord,* feeling very preoccupied. What if what she was saying really worked? Could we honestly still expect God to speak to us individually as He spoke to the prophets of old?

The possibilities were exciting! I could hardly wait to get home and see if it worked for me! I made sure I'd fulfilled the conditions outlined in her talk: There was no one I needed to forgive, Jesus truly was the Lord of my life, I made sure I was repentant for any sins in my past, and I truly desired to seek Him above all else. My motives were right.

With pen in hand, and note pad ready, I said: "OK, Lord, I'm ready . . . if you are." I began to

Speak Lord

write! Oh, I don't mean I was suddenly overtaken by some supernatural force that used my hand to form letters on paper. (That is automatic writing, and I believe that to be a manifestation of the occult. I wanted no part of that!) Well, it was supernatural all right, but it seemed so natural to me (and it still does). The Lord filled my mind with His words! I didn't stop for a minute to think of what to say next; I didn't have to. The words just flowed, pouring from His mind and heart to my mind and heart . . . and pen!

At first I really couldn't comprehend anything other than wondering if I had uncovered some latent, hidden talent within me! But after weeks of meeting with Him in the morning and receiving a different message each time—all beautiful and all meaningful, either to me or to someone else—it soon became evident that this could not be coming from me! Each morning I received a profoundly pertinent message that would, that day, meet my need or the needs of someone else. If the message was meant for someone else, I was led to give it to them and their response was always such that I knew their Heavenly Father and mine had arranged another divine encounter!

In spite of all this, I suddenly began to doubt and be fearful that this may not be truly the Lord doing this, that it may be some trick of the devil or a trick my mind was playing on me. My prayer was fervent: "Father, if this is not from *You, please* take it away from me, I don't want to play games in Your name; but if this truly is You, then allow a sign to reassure me."

In that same still, small voice in my spirit that I had already learned to expect and love, He told me I would receive a package that day and that would be my sign.

I waited in eager anticipation for a package all day, but none arrived. When I got home from work later that day I was disconsolate, distressed, disturbed, and feeling slightly deranged! Had I been imagining the whole thing? Was this really just a crazy figment of my overactive imagination? If so, then surely I must be crazy! Puzzled and upset, I climbed into my bed and just stared up at the ceiling. Doubts of every description assailed me! What would become of me in this mentally unbalanced condition?

The peal of the doorbell interrupted my disturbing thoughts! For some reason, I checked the clock (even that was ordained by the Lord; I don't usually look at the clock when the doorbell rings!) It was exactly 7 o'clock (seven the—Lord's number!). Upon answering the door, I found a deliveryman standing there with a package for me in his hands!

The next thing I remember was holding a box closely in my arms and just walking around the house praising the Lord!

It must have been fifteen minutes before I opened that box! When I finally did open it, I discovered a lovely ceramic dove, sent to me by

Speak Lord

some friends I had not heard from in years! (Could that dove have been a symbol to me of the coming of the Holy Spirit?) Rarely, if ever, do I receive packages by mail, not even at Christmas—and this was July! I knew then that this precious package was really a gift from my Heavenly Father in loving, understanding assurance for one of his present day doubting Thomases!

The Lord is faithful, and although there are still times when I have doubted, He has been patient and explained that, in a way, these messages are from me, as He is in me, and my spirit is joined to His Spirit, so what He tells me does get filtered through my very finite mind. In essence, though, it is He, our precious Lord and Savior, reaching down to touch the lives of those of His who would stop, come apart, and listen, just as Samuel did so long ago: "Speak, Lord, for Your servant is listening" (1 Samuel 3:9).

I pray you will be blessed and edified by this random sampling of messages I've put together out of the thousands I've received through the years. Many were not meant for me but were given to me to share with someone to whom the Lord would lead me that day; someone who, as I would discover, desperately needed this "now" word from their loving Heavenly Father, clearly addressing a situation they were experiencing at that time. I believe many of the words written here were meant to speak directly to you, too. The Lord knows what your need is today. As you read, al-

Carol Brown

low Him to speak to you, meet your need, and minister His love, His comfort, His correction, His strength, and His healing into your life. May the Lord use these words to bless you today!

Introduction

Do you feel alone? Do you feel like your prayers are bouncing off the ceiling? Do you want a closer relationship with your Heavenly Father? *Let Him tell you how!*

After the prayer, after the praise, after the worship, do you still feel like you're not quite there? What comes next? You listen!

Let Him show you how He wants to speak to you. God will always speak to you through the Bible, if you are tuned in to Him. If you have the gift of public speaking, if you are a good listener, or if you just plain like to talk, He may speak to you as a verbal word, even an audible word. God may speak to you through a prophecy, a speaker, your own words, or through someone else's words. If you love to read, God may chose to speak to you through a letter from a friend, a book, or even through something you read in the newspaper. I love to write, so that's where He meets me. But, of course, our Sovereign Lord can speak to us any way He wants . . . if only we are listening.

How can we feel confident that what we hear is from the Lord and not from the devil in an attempt to deceive us?

1. Does it confirm what the Bible says? (God will never contradict His word.)
2. Does it make you love God more, feel closer to Him, and look forward to meeting with Him often?
3. Does it bring peace, a sense of security? Correction maybe, but never condemnation!
4. Does it cause a sense of connection to God and a greater inner strength?
5. Does it make you desire to please and serve Him more?

If what you heard was from the enemy, the opposite of these would be true!

How do you know these are not just from your subconscious or from your own over active imagination? Time will take care of that! After thousands of messages (some of which I have picked at random to include in this book), I am convinced that, although these words come through my spirit, the source is the Source of all: our Lord. The One Who has promised that "My sheep hear My voice" (John

10:27). You are His sheep if you are His and follow Him, so you should *expect* to hear His voice.

This all may take time, take fine tuning, take patience, but I can promise you it will be well worth the effort.

You are about to set sail on the most exciting adventure of your life! It's fun, it's fulfilling, it's fruitful . . . and it's fantastic.

—Carol Brown
Orlando, Florida
CBROWN3346@msn.com

Don't be dismayed, and do not be afraid. Why shouldn't I speak to you? You are My own beloved child! I have sought you out and claimed you for My very own. You have responded to My love, and now I seek communion with you. Why do you marvel that I speak to you? Do you not speak to your children? You are My child, I am your Father.

Write down what comes to your mind (you will know soon enough if the message is from Satan or from Me). You are fearful that it may be all in your mind. Well, that is partly true, because I am in you, and you are in Me, so My messages for you do come from My Spirit to your spirit, translated through your mind and put into the words you write. It is for this reason that some of My children have My word come to them in early English, for this is how they perceive it should be. The thoughts are Mine, the translation is yours! Be at peace with this.

There is a time coming, and shortly will be, when there will be a great awakening. At that time I will tear the blinders off the eyes of those who cannot see. I will pour the oil of My Spirit into hearts that are hard and those hearts will be softened toward Me.

There is a day coming, and shortly will be, when those who cry "nonsense" to the word of God will fall on their faces before Me and cry "mercy."

There is an hour coming, and shortly will be, when My people, face to face, will pour out their hearts and minds and love to one another and then, in one accord, turn and face Me . . . radiant with the glow of love and forgiveness . . . and pour out their praise and adoration to Me.

That is the time, beloved, when I will gather you into My arms. The harvest will be plentiful, and there will be rejoicing throughout the face of the earth.

That is the day I will finish that for which I came the first time: I will bring to completion My work of salvation; redemption will be complete, and I will see My final act of restoration come to pass. That is the day I gather you, as a hen gathers her chicks, and present you to My Father . . . My Bride . . . adorned for the feast!

Yes, I have dealt bountifully with you since you gave Me that right. Yes, I have blessed you, but you have not yet begun to comprehend what I intend to do for you. I love you fiercely! I love you intently! I love you with a single mindedness that excludes all thought of anything less. You are forgiven, cleansed, redeemed, renewed, restored, sanctified. You are wholly Mine . . . and I treasure you! Be ever aware of this and walk in the peace, love, and joy that knowledge affords.

I paid too high a price for you not to treasure you! I paid that price knowing exactly all that it would cost Me, yet I gave no thought to refusing to pay for you . . . even knowing you as I do, I still wanted you that much! Try your best to understand all that means, for I want you to truly understand how I feel about you.

Walk now in the fullness of all the joy that brings; let it put a spring in your step, a smile on your face, and an outpouring of that joy out of your innermost being.

Yes, beloved of Mine, walk in an ever growing knowledge and understanding of all it means to be engulfed in perfect love, and then pray that others will come to know that same Love . . . standing at the door of their hearts . . . knocking . . . waiting . . . just for them.

Speak Lord

There is a sweet breeze of restoration blowing over you this day. This is a day of refreshment, of breaking the bonds of unholy alliance.

The freedom that has always been rightfully yours has been bound. I loose you now, for the time is right. You have learned what I wanted you to learn. I will not allow your submission, your death of self, your obedience, to cross the line.

Quenching the spirit does not only mean the Holy Spirit, it can mean your spirit too. My Holy word forbids anyone to quench your spirit. You are as dear and as valuable to Me as anyone else. You have sat at the bottom of the table long enough, I say to you now: "Friend, come up higher" (Luke 14:10). There will be no threat now of pride's destructive invasion, for now you know who you truly are: A sinner saved by grace.

Now, I call you to walk in the role of the victor . . . the head, not the tail . . . a child of the King of Kings, an ambassador of the kingdom.

Now, My precious child, go . . . and be who you really are.

As it was in the flesh, so you have been born of Me in the Spirit. As a newborn babe, you had to be washed (in the water of baptism), and made to breathe fresh, life-giving air (the breath of life the Holy Spirit imparted). You had to be given new clothes to wear (My robe of righteousness). You were fed (nourished by My word). All the needs of the newborn baby were met so your body and your spirit could grow strong. One day it came time for you to step out on your own, and your Father had to take His hand away or you would never have learned to walk on your own. But His hand was always ready, waiting to catch you if you fell. A baby falls many times at first, but does a loving parent discard the toddler, give up on her and have no more to do with her if she falls? Of course not! A loving parent will always lift her back up on her feet with a smile of compassion and encouragement. Because he is always there she learns to trust him and know that he will be there the next time. So she takes his hand in confidence, looks into his eyes, and, seeing only love there, trusts him to put her back on her feet.

How very much does physical growth parallel the spiritual! They both take time, they both need help: someone to love, forgive, and restore. I am all that to you.

Speak Lord

Blessed are they who put their trust in Me. Not in money, not in land, not in government, nor material wealth, nor position; but blessed are they who acknowledge Me as their only source, these are the ones I can truly trust, these are the ones I can truly bless.

Look to your job as your source of supply and you tie My hands. Look only to Me, and I will use your job, or anything else I choose, to bless you and to meet your needs.

I am the Alpha and the Omega, the beginning and the end of all things. I am your all in all . . . in everything . . . for everything. Outside of Me there is nothing but doom. In Me is pure joy, light and life and love.

Rid your life of everything that is not of Me. Every area of your life that does not give Me glory is an area where My life force is being blocked from flowing freely into you. Once you rid your life of all those blocks then, and only then, will I be free to move unobstructed, to heal, deliver, and bless you in every area of your life. This is the way it was always meant to be, and this is My desire for My own.

"It is your Father's good pleasure to give you the kingdom" (Luke 12:32).

Endurance does not necessarily mean a great physical pressure: running a long distance race, being tortured for your faith, and resisting the temptation to give in to the tormentors. These are the sort of things one thinks of when they think of the words: "He who endures to the end will be saved" (Matt. 10:22). You have a mental picture of being tied to a stake, a fire lit, and your enemies standing over you saying: "Deny Christ, or we set you afire."

Endurance can also mean getting up every morning, long before you want to, into a cold house, going to a job you don't always enjoy very much, and doing that every day of your life, knowing it will probably be so for the next twenty years.

Endurance is patience when you feel the most impatient; it is lovingly caring for the most unlovable in the name of Christ; it is waiting on the Lord when it seems like nothing is going your way and suffering in silence when all you want to do is complain.

Endurance is standing strong in your faith when it seems everything around you is crumbling and no one understands you . . . or really cares.

Doing these sort of things and offering them up as a gift of sacrifice, this too is endurance. "He who endures to the end will be saved." (Matt. 24:13).

Speak Lord

Go forth in peace to love and serve Me. Be faithful always, know My love, live in the constant awareness that I am closer to you than your skin . . . closer than your breath.

I am an all-encompassing God. You either want Me or you don't. If you want Me, you get all of Me, not just fragments from time to time. If you mean business with Me, your ministry will be your life—not a job.

Do you want to go all the way with Me . . . or do you want to hang onto other people's shirttails on the brink and never take the plunge? I know your answer, and I mean business with you too!

I am even now separating the wheat from the chaff. Soon I will no longer abide fence straddlers. Man must either be all for Me . . . or he must get off the fence and join the ranks of Satan. I will bless you eternally for your unwavering choice.

Be brave—I will make you strong. Be patient—I will give you a quiet spirit. Be happy—I will give you joy. Be radiant—for the Sun of Righteousness forever shines within you.

This walk is a walk of surrender.

Lay down your arms at the foot of the cross . . . all the carnal weapons of defense and false protection.

Cast aside the deadly arrows of the enemy that cause you to react in response to others with thoughts of rejection, rebellion, pride, and hurt instead of selfless love. Lay these deadly arrows down once and for all, and never stoop to pick them up again.

Lay aside the heavy artillery that weighs you down: The feelings of inadequacy, of frustration, of uselessness. Turn away from fear of failure and from fear of the future.

Trust Me to see you through the tight places . . . have I ever failed you?

Lay aside the darts of criticism and judgment, the poisonous darts that burn and fester and kill.

Lay down your arms . . . and come and rest in mine.

Speak Lord

All I have given you, turn and give away.

I give anew, afresh. Never fear emptiness after giving out, for only as you pour yourself out can I fill you in a deeper way than ever before.

Each time I fill you, your capacity to receive increases by the very act of your giving, so each time you are able to receive more.

Be patient with those who are not where you are, as I have been patient with you . . . watching you grow, helping in every way I could, yet never pushing nor demanding . . . only loving . . . and waiting . . . as you received, drop by drop, what I wanted to give you ocean by ocean!

You still have a long way to go, but now I can start pouring in more from larger vessels . . . no more drops, but rivers of living water!

Everything you are feeling now is but a foretaste of the things to come. Your joy is only a mere reflection of the far deeper joys awaiting you. Your peace only a foreshadowing of that deep abiding peace you will experience eternally abiding in Me.

The beauty of nature that you now enjoy so much will be dramatically intensified when the true nature that is in you is unhampered by the things that now cloud your view. Now you see as in a glass darkly, but then . . . oh, then beloved, you will know, even as you are known! What a day that will be!

You are looking at the negative now, then you will see the full-blown picture in all its color, in all its radiance, and in all its perfect beauty.

Then your mind will be free to soar to heights unimagined now. Then I will take you beyond the limitations of your finite mind, and you will know . . . and you will share . . . infinity with Me. Wait for that with bated breath and a heart full of excitement! Just know you haven't even scratched the surface!

Speak Lord

What is an act of faith? To go through the motions "as if it were" . . . and leave the rest to Me; to step out into the darkness; to make a move first. . . and to *expect* to hear from me, not just to sit back and wait to see if you will hear from Me.

To commit yourself is to step out on a limb where there is no turning back, no alternate way. Either I come through, or you fall. Beloved, I do not cut down limbs My children climb out on because of their faith in Me! Complete trust: "Commit your ways unto the Lord" (Psalm 37:5) without fear—in complete trust. Give Me the problem, the burden, the care.

Throw Me the ball, I haven't fumbled yet! I never will. You will never make the goal on your own from where you stand now, but give it to the One with the perfect score, and you will always come out a winner! You are on My team . . . and we are the winners! Remember that, and when the opposing team makes a score, don't let it bother you . . . it is the final score that counts!

Why do you fear failure? Is it not because you do not truly believe Me when I tell you that "All things work together for good to those who love the Lord" (Romans 8:28)? You have given Me your life; *am* I not capable of handling it? If you cannot see a purpose, nor a design, does it mean there is none? I am in charge. I *am* all-powerful in a life fully yielded to Me . . . and above all I love you. Rest, trust, and be free. No one has ever truly come to Me and been turned away.

You have offered your life to Me . . . I have accepted your offer. Now, as I begin to remake you into the person I had intended you to be from the creation of the world, there is much to be undertaken. Through acting in your sin nature and responding as carnal man to life, you have formed thought patterns and habits that must be broken, must be reversed, and you must be led to function in a whole new way . . . the way you were created to function. A lot of this process has brought pain, and you have not always understood why you are in certain situations.

Remember, too, not every situation you are in is for your blessing alone, for I use you in the lives of many. One day you will hear: "Thank you, you helped me to get here." That, beloved, will make it all worthwhile!

Don't imagine yourself with any one ministry. You are to be My hands extended to offer the cup of cold water, to be My channel for healing . . . to wear many hats . . . to be there for whatever the need may be. Don't become set into a mold; be flexible . . . only then can I mold you.

I have not called you to be a healer; I have called you to speak My word of healing. I have not called you to a deliverance ministry; I have called you to speak deliverance in My Name. Under the power of My Spirit and in the authority of My Name, the forces of evil are subject to you and must obey. I have not called you to save the world, but to speak of the Savior of the world to those who have ears to hear (I will show you who they are).

I have called you to be all things to all people in My Name, in My authority. You have My power of attorney. I commission you: use it and don't be afraid.

I will cause to come into being that which has been created by faith. So, use your faith to speak My word . . . then leave the outcome to Me.

I say to you now, My child . . . relax. Enjoy Me. Don't take your Christian walk so seriously! Be free to love your life in Me. Be at home in the ways of your Lord.

"In My presence there is fullness of joy" (Ps. 16:11), and only in My presence can this be found. Seek to be ever in My presence, and joy will find you there.

Don't try to run to catch up with those ahead of you, and don't try to pull at those behind you. It is not for you to judge who is ahead of you and who is behind you. See that you are where you should be and leave the judgment to Me. Speak only what is given you to say, and let the perfect Judge do the rest.

Do not fear failure. Do not fear man. You will be given all . . . and more . . . of what you need. I only call you to stay close to Me and find your rest in Me. You don't have to have all the answers . . . only know that I do.

Do what is given you to do (you will not know what this is unless you stay close to Me) and then go and do it in trust. I will not fail you.

After having done all . . . just stand . . . and enjoy Me.

"I am come that they may have life and have it abundantly" (John 10:10). The closer you come to Me, the more abundant your life. My provisions are boundless! It is not the quantity of time spent with Me; it is the quality of that time. You can spend hours trying to "touch God," when I am already here! You need only appropriate what is already yours. You can spend days seeking a supernatural manifestation and end up with nothing more than a frustrated feeling of failure, or you can spend five minutes yielded to how I want to reveal Myself to you . . . and come away aglow with the Spirit!

A life yielded to Me must be your goal; an attitude of communion with Me always, at all times, in the busiest moments of your day, locked in with Me in the secret place of your heart . . . short "arrow prayers" acknowledging your dependence upon the God of your creation to whom you owe each breath. That yielded life, that acceptance of dependence, those quick "I love You, Jesus" words; the times in indecision when your first thought is: "What do You want, Lord?" these things are precious in My sight, and through them you sometimes grow faster than spending long hours concentrating on "seeking God." It is My Spirit Who gives the growth . . . not any effort on your part.

You are coming to the time in your life when you will strive to be in constant communion with Me. This will be your final stage of Christian growth in the earthly realm.

You have just begun this walk. How long it will take for a perfect union is not the question, for that will not be in this phase of your existence. That perfection of union will come in the next life for you.

What counts now is your constant practice of My presence. Dwell on Me, dwell in Me, dwell with Me. "Let this mind be in you which is also in Christ Jesus" (Phil. 2:5).

Practice My presence.

Long hours of meditation can be beautiful; they can bless, inspire, and nourish you, but they are not the secret keys to spiritual maturity—obedience and yieldedness are.

Speak Lord

So you want to be an instrument in the hands of the Great Physician?

You know that instruments used by physicians must be precision instruments. Suppose something went wrong with the surgical scissors and they didn't close? Great care goes into the making of these instruments to insure they will perform as they should. They are put through great pressure and heat. Do you want that? There are some instruments that are not as useful and are not as well made. Do you want that?

I will take you as far as you want to go. I will use you as much as you are willing to be used. But to do that I will have to make you fit for the job. It may mean doing more than you think—or it may mean less; whichever way it goes, are you willing to see it through? Only you can say.

I need all the precision instruments I can get, for there is much surgery to be done.

What kind of instrument do you want to be? I love you; I want you to be useful to Me. You will get all the help you need. Give me your answer . . . there is no turning back. I will bless you, and your joy will be full. You are in My hands now. A good physician takes a firm grip on his instruments and holds them securely in the palm of his hand.

How pleasant is the valley I have for you to walk through now! The beauty there . . . the sweet ripe fruit for you to eat! There no sorrow will befall you . . . only My perfect peace, joy, comfort, and love.

I have many blessings to bless you with.

This is not a valley of sorrow nor pain, but a valley of rest and consolation. It is there I wait for you even now and call you to Myself. There you will find only what will make your heart glad; you will welcome the cool refreshment it affords.

I call you now to come into that valley. It is Satan's valley that holds sadness, depression, and pain. My valleys are soft and cool with still waters—cool and refreshing, for you to drink. The delight of the banquet I offer you will invigorate and strengthen you.

My valley holds rest for the weary, comfort for those who hurt, refreshment for the worn and frazzled. The healing, reviving balm of My valley is waiting for you . . . and you don't have to travel far to go into the secret place of the Most High . . . our secret place. Just sit still and go to that quiet place in your heart and keep your eyes on Me. I am waiting there for you now.

You have a built-in survival kit in the very depth of your being. The contents of this kit, if you were to examine them, would be:

1. The knowledge of Who God is: This is the antiseptic. Once you know Who is on your side in the battle, you need never fear infiltration of the enemy like germs into a wound.
2. The knowledge of who you are: This is the medicine for the wound. The healing of your wound will occur when you take your rightful place in My family . . . a blood-washed, clean, sanctified, heir of salvation; with the power in you to withstand any attack . . . to absorb My life as a healing balm into your spirit.
3. The final ingredient is: My word in your life: This is the bandage. This is what seals the wound and protects it from further hurt. "He sent His word and healed them" (Psalm 107:20), not only to bandage the wound, but to serve as a defensive weapon to stave off further attack.

Now, beloved, you are fully protected. Go into battle . . . go into victory!

How precious to Me are those moments you spend in My presence! How very much I desire to bless you with all spiritual blessings in heavenly places. "I will restore unto you the years the swarming locust has eaten" (Joel 2:25). I will carve upon you a new name. I will create within you a new life—in every sense of the word: A new physical life—a new way of thinking—a new spiritual life.

You are going far with Me, but do not think of that as the doorway to tribulation! My saints may have tribulation, yes, but so do the godless. The difference is My saints have My strength and My promise of protection and My assurance of victory; the tribulation is but a slight, momentary affliction; whereas to the lost the same situation would be a disaster.

I supply the strength. All you need to do is keep your eyes on Me—not on the circumstance.

I have delivered you out of far worse situations than this one. I will set your feet on solid ground. I am the Rock on which you are firmly and immovably set.

You hold the key—use it. Use it to open doors that lead to where you want to go; when you open each door you will find I have gone ahead of you, and you will find Me standing there waiting for you.

Speak Lord

I am calling you to a new kind of stillness—a stillness you can feel with every fiber of your being, a calm . . . even in the midst of the raging storm.

This stillness is a precursor—a preparation for that which is to come. I am preparing your heart for abiding in My presence. You cannot be anything but still when you are cradled in My arms, when you are basking in My glory, when My radiance floods in and around you.

You have walked in tumult, both of body and mind, for most of your adult life. The dry, parched areas of your life, the tumult—like a fire within, is now being quenched by the water of My word. The cool wind of the Spirit of God blows over you now . . . revitalizing you, refreshing and restoring you, and you will be flooded with My presence.

So, beloved, bask now in My glory. Take joy from My heart of love for you. Rest in My peace and practice My presence for, you see, the day is coming (even faster than you think) when all My promises to you will, in one fell swoop, be yours.

So, just for now, "Be still, and know that I am God" (Psalm 46:10).

I have planted within you the tree of life. The seed, buried deep in the soil of your soul at salvation, has taken root and is growing steadily. You are allowing Me to water this young plant from the rivers of living water. You have welcomed the Light of the World to spread His sunshine and, in the warmth of His Love, the baby seedling grows strong and tall.

Now the tree puts forth blossoms and, as happens so often in the spring of life, the harsh winds blow many of those blossoms to the ground. Is this a reason to give up and cut down the tree, My little one? I prune My young trees . . . but I never cut them down. Look instead at the strong remaining blossoms as they mature into small green fruit. Your lessons in patience become the focal point. Wait for the full maturity of My fruit, and when they are fully ripened I will pick from your tree. All you have to do is wait. I do not pick green fruit, neither do I allow the fruit to rot on the tree.

The reason for your sojourn on Planet Earth is so that you can fully mature, so that you may become more and more conformed into the image of Christ your King. This present life is a school, preparing you for eternity. Pass your tests, beloved, and you will not have to repeat them.

The Carpenter from Nazareth still needs His tools. Sometimes He needs a hammer to drive a point home. To hold things together He may need a vise, or a good strong nail. He needs pieces of pipe or tubes. No matter what they are, all His tools are necessary, but He can only use them if they are available to Him.

Just be available and I will use you. I am not looking for ability . . . but availability . . . I will create within you the ability.

I have created you exactly the way I want you . . . to be what I want you to be and to do what I want you to do.

Suppose the nail decided it didn't want to be a nail anymore, but wanted to be a wrench, when what the Carpenter needed was nothing more or less than a nail! Be whatever it is I need at any given time . . . not what you think you would be best equipped for. I will equip you to function when, where, and how you are needed.

Let your confidence be in Me, not in your ability. Merely will to will the will of God . . . and be available.

There are passages in the dwelling place I have for you that lead into different rooms.

There is the living room: here you spend a lot of your time just living out the everyday chores and what you may consider the mundane areas of each day. The passageway to this room is strewn with lessons of endurance, patience, and longsuffering.

Then there is the den: this is the recreational area of your life. This room is filled with areas of temptations, broken dreams, unfulfilled ambitions, and dreams. This passageway will lead you to turn to Me more than ever before and find in Me the answers you seek.

The kitchen area: this is where you are fed and nourished, where you will grow strong in Me through the water of the word and the fruit of the Spirit.

There is the library: here is where you "study to show yourself approved" (2 Tim. 2:15). The passageway through this area calls for lessons in perseverance, concentration, determination, and self control.

The passageway that leads to the bedroom area is sometimes the hardest to follow, for it leads through areas that test your faith, and sometimes this passageway becomes very dark; but, just when you feel like you have lost your way you make a sudden turn, and find yourself in a place of perfect

Speak Lord

rest, contentment and peace, where the Lover of your soul waits to comfort you and forever enfold you in His waiting arms.

Welcome to the dwelling place I have for you! You have made it through the passageways, and you know your way around. Now . . . make yourself at home, eternally to be with Me in My dwelling place . . . seated with Me in heavenly places forevermore.

There are paths through the gardens you cannot yet follow. But don't be disheartened, for the paths will still be there to be followed . . . at a later time.

I know how you feel, and I am watching you and watching over you. I won't take you through byways that are too difficult for you. I am leading you home the way that is best for you.

Don't try to follow in the pathway of another's walk with Me. Everyone's pathway is different, and everyone needs to travel their special route at their own pace . . . but it is the same destination. Just keep on in the way you are going. Don't run ahead of Me . . . don't fall back . . . you will get there. Let Me be your guide, and I will see to it that you don't get lost!

Picture the beauty of nature in all its splendor, absorb the scents of nature all around you . . . the soft caress of balmy breezes, the sun's gentle rays warming you inside and out.

Picture the high and lofty mountains rolling gently to the pure, clear aquamarine sea. Watch a little ant busily going about its business . . . I am in charge of both . . . ponder on this.

Picture My loving you through nature, through all the things that are manifested in one lovely flower, in the brilliant or muted colors of a bird, in the playfulness of a kitten, in the energy of a small dog. See My love for you in all of nature.

If you think your home here on earth is so beautiful—imagine how much more beautiful is the life I have ahead for you!

This life is only the negative . . . the glorious finished photo will soon be revealed to you . . . and you will almost explode with joy!

Speak Lord

Has a sparrow ever fallen and I have not seen? And if a sparrow, then all birds, and if all birds . . . then all animals, fish and, yes, even the smallest ant does not go unknown, unnoticed, and alone.

How much more you, child of My love? *How much more you!*

Picture a lovely garden, in bloom with every beautiful flower you can imagine . . . picture a tiny cardinal hopping on a limb, picture a little squirrel sitting up and begging . . . just for your enjoyment! See the regal lion standing proudly, as though he were aware of his title, "king of the jungle." Picture, too, a column of tiny ants, busily going about their business. See the lofty pinnacles of snow capped mountains. . . the mighty oceans of the world . . . their vastness; think of how much they all must weigh . . . yet I hold them all in the palm of My hand!

I hold the mountains . . . I hold the oceans . . . I hold the ant . . . and, yes, beloved . . . I hold you.

As long as you live, there will be valleys you will have to go through on your journey home. Remember a valley is always a place between two mountains! When you come down from a mountaintop experience, it is likely you will find yourself in a valley. But look ahead, keep your eyes fixed on the road ahead. You will soon be on top of that next mountain! Never lose hope; only trust, wait . . . and obey. I always see you through, and you will be more nearly conformed to the image of My Son when you get to the other side.

How can you know how to resist temptation unless you have been tempted? How do you learn to love your enemies if you never have any? How can you win if there is never a battle? In Me you are more than a conqueror! "In all these things we are more than conquerors through Him Who loved us" (Romans 8:37).

I will do all that is necessary to bring any situation around to become a blessing for you, if you will but give it to Me. Whatever troubles you, lay it at the foot of My cross; you were never meant to bear these burdens alone; they are too heavy for you. Give them to Me and I will take them from you.

Speak Lord

There are some of My children who are living this earthly life like a horse with blinders on. They see only the end of the trail (salvation) . . . which is good, the goal is there, but they miss all the beauty along the way, all the gifts I have for them while they are still in this phase of their lives. They never stop to smell the flowers!

There can be no sunshine without the Son. So many try to live in My provisions without living in Me. So many try to appropriate My gifts, but turn their backs on the Giver.

Point them to Me. Show them the Source of all they want and need. Show them that to live without Me is like trying to stay warm by hiding in the shadow a house casts instead of going through the door to the warmth within.

I have commissioned you . . . go and do as I have commanded: Be Me to those around you; for to many you are the closest they have ever been to Me. Be ever aware of this.

You ask: "Is Jesus truly the *only* way?" Beloved, if there could have been another way *would I not have taken it? Would I not have spared My beloved Son?*

For the latter rains will surely come, the earth will be flooded with My Spirit, and the earth will experience physical floods. The earth will be shaken by spiritual warfare, and the power of God will shake all that can be shaken . . . and there will be great earthquakes. Spiritual darkness will bring forth physical darkness, and the light of the Son, and the light of the sun cut off. For every spiritual event there will be a physical counterpart. This is true in every area.

Think about this, and write down all you can think of and pray that this revelation will be understood and take hold and that My people will apply this principle to their lives.

Whatever happens in the spiritual realm is manifested in the material. Watch this principle; learn how it operates, and use it to bring forth My will in your life, and pray that others will do the same.

When this is done, the glory of the Lord will cover the earth as the waters cover the sea.

From you, beloved, will spring forth My living water, fresher by far than the clearest springs from the loftiest mountains on earth; for you have climbed the mountain and have tasted the fresh mountain water of the Spirit. Now it shall overflow within you and spring forth and cascade down the mountainside, richly flowing in abundance . . . fresh, crystal clear, clean, pure, sweet, and holy.

You will comprehend Peter's desire to express all that he felt on the Mount of Transfiguration, for you will want to hold these moments forever. But don't be afraid to let them go, as they are only the beginning of all I have for you!

The things of earth will become more and more the backdrop, and the things of the Spirit more and more the real world to you. You will never lose touch with reality as you know it now, but it will be put in its proper prospective.

Press on to the high calling in Christ Jesus. Be faithful, in and out of season, walk circumspectly before Me. "Study to show yourself approved, a workman rightly dividing the word of God" (2 Tim. 2:15).

Then, beloved, hold on tight . . . for your present mountains will become as bumps in the road as you grow and as you go . . . from glory to glory.

As I give to you, go and give to others. You are to be My conduit. If you try to hold on to what I give you, it will turn to dust in your hands. You must give in order to receive more.

The life I give unto you is a spring, not a lake. It must be constantly pouring out, or it will stagnate and bring death to the heart.

Many wonder why there is so little real peace and joy in their lives and yet, when I nudge them to reach out beyond their borders, they draw back in fear, or worse—distaste. Real joy comes with giving.

If you want My joy, it has to be on My terms. It is not up to you to pick what you will, or will not, do. Be the glove . . . allow Me to be the hand. Abandonment is the key.

This is not a set of "how-to" rules; it is an art learned only through the school of obedience. Do what is set before you. Then you get the rest, then you get the joy. Refuse to do what is set before you, and in that realm you go no further. Do what I have told you to do, and the next step will be plain. Many wonder why they don't hear from Me. When did they hear last? What did they do about it?

What you call a fear of disobedience can actually be a fear of failure. Disobedience is an unruly spirit that is rooted in selfishness. Fear of failure is a by product of rejection and is only dealt with through trust and obedience to My Spirit. See how I never fail you? See how I provide when all of your other resources have failed? Trust Me, and leave the outcome to Me, and fear of failure will have no hold on your life anymore.

I speak a promise to all those afraid of failure: "Your strength is made perfect in weakness" (2 Cor. 12:9). This is one of the most powerful promises in the Bible and one of the least followed.

Only as you discover that I always come through when you cannot, will fear of failure and rejection be absorbed into My healing love. This kind comes out no other way.

So don't be afraid to fail at what I call you to do. I call you because I know, in Me . . . you can.

I speak to the storm in your life and I say: "Peace, be still." Once the storm has abated, I want you to survey the damage. Has water leaked into your house and weakened the foundation? Has wind blown the roof off your house? Has lightning set fire to your home?

Now is the time to take stock and think about rebuilding. I, your "Insurance Adjuster," do not condemn your house, but rather I provide the means for you to rebuild and, yes, to make your home better than ever. Your house, your life, is Mine. I am your Cornerstone. Let us begin there.

The Cornerstone is now firmly in place. Now ask the Holy Spirit (Who comes to you as wind, water, and fire) to recreate what the enemy has destroyed. Do not look to the past, thereby making the same mistakes all over again, but consider yourself destroyed and completely rebuilt by the "Master Builder" Himself. "You are no longer your own. . . you have been bought with a price" (1 Cor. 6:19–20). . . the highest price ever paid for anything!

Now make My house a place of worship, dedicated to Me. A house where I can be comfortable, where I can call home; where no evil thing abides. I cannot . . . I will not, share My house with Satan. I cannot live with his trophies around Me.

When your house is flooded with the water of the word, all filth is removed. The germs of immorality, hatred, lies, and deception are killed by the fire of the Spirit. The wind of the Spirit blows in fresh ideas, fresh ideals, fresh desires . . . and the old is blown away.

Now your house is My temple. Now I can rule and reign in your heart. Now there are no more impurities: no more dishonesty, no more hurt, no more unforgiveness, no more hate, no more bitterness, no more disrespect, no more disobedience. Now I can move in your life in ways you never comprehended before.

The enemy will always try to reenter. He will knock, he will ring the doorbell, he will call on the phone, he will try to enter by TV, by the Internet, the radio, by mail . . . any way he can. He will try to enter through the eye gate (through what you see), by the ear gate (by what you hear), through people, or through your own mind. But, remember Who owns the house now; and when Satan knocks, just ask Me, the Owner, to open the door. I know how to deal with him!

The call to ministry is not so much a glorious call to arms (although those times do come) so much as it is a simple call to take the next step.

If you begin your day with an openness to discern My will, you will find it. It will not be hard to find, but it can be hard to do, especially at first. It will be something that only I can do through you. But do not despair. Compared to the life of sin and rebellion, "My yoke is easy and My burden is light" (Matt. 11:30).

During the course of the day you run across many different people from many different backgrounds with varied ideas of how best to get through their lives. You must learn how to treat each one so that the source of their need is tapped, so that you will be able to really reach them. You may be brimming over with things you want to say to them, but if those things are not what they are ready to hear, you can do more harm than good, for you may be trying to force them into a phase of life that they are not yet equipped to handle. People must be met at their point of need. I do not pick green fruit! Discern what needs to be said or done to properly minister to each individual. Let your spirit reach out and touch their spirits . . . My Spirit will show the way.

Speak Lord

The, song in your heart is put there by My joy. I am the Composer of your song; your spirit, the choir director . . . your heart, the voice of the song.

It is a song of worship, a song of praise, and I am well pleased at the rendition . . . it is just how the Composer intended it to be sung. I "joy over you with singing" (Zeph. 3:17). I rejoice in your joy!

You have been faithful over little, I will make you faithful over much. Lean on Me and not on your own understanding, and let not your heart be troubled.

When I prepare a pathway for you it means that I have already gone before and removed the obstacles, so when you get there your path will be clear.

So, sing your song, My child; I am enjoying every moment of it! It is the song of the ages. One day you will sing it to its fullest . . . with full accompaniment: the angelic hosts of heaven, and it will be a magnificent song . . . an eternal song. I have placed this song in your heart, so sing it loud and clear: a new song, a never ending song, a beautiful song, a song written just for you, from the Composer, with His love.

Carol Brown

𝓔ach one of My children is given a light at the moment of their salvation. How brightly that light shines depends upon the battery, and how strong and powerful that battery is depends upon you. Do you constantly charge your battery? Do you feed on My word, persevere in prayer and communion with My people? Do you know this is the way to charge your battery?

There is much that puts added strain on your battery, aside from the daily routine. When you intercede you pour out, when you counsel you pour out, when you serve you pour out. In so many ways you are constantly putting a strain on this battery of yours, but this is one battery that will not wear out, but rather it grows stronger each time it is charged!

So, come for re-charging often, and your Light (Christ in you) will burn forever brightly. Satan would that he could diminish that light through feelings of inadequacy, but only answer him like this: "Yes, I know I am inadequate, (agree with your adversary, Matt. 5:25) but yet I am adequate with the adequacy of Jesus . . . and He is my all-sufficiency."

Speak Lord

For this I came: that all men and every nation should have access to the throne of the Father. The cross is the doorway to the throne room. Many stand in front and gaze in wonder, but until they go beyond the cross and enter in, they are not in the Kingdom of God. Many will say on that day: "Lord, I have always believed in you." Yes, and so does their father, the devil!

You must go beyond . . . go past belief . . . go past the cross: "Yes, Jesus died for Me; I believe that, and I now receive the consequences of His death. I enter into that death with Him. I have died with Him; I was in Him at the point of death. I believe Jesus rose again. I identify with His resurrection, and I rise with Him to newness of life. Moreover, I believe Jesus ascended into heaven as the Victor King. I identify with that ascension, and at that point, whether I understand it or not, I believe I, too, ascended with Him and sit with Him forever in heavenly places (Eph. 2: 6).

Since now I am seated with Christ in heavenly places, I am outside the reach of Satan . . . he has no power over me, for he cannot invade God's heavenly places . . . and I am safe, safe in My Father's arms."

The life force that is governing your life has its core in the eternal spring that was from the beginning. You are joined for all eternity to the Giver of life Himself.

The life current that runs through your body is that same current that emanates from the Father to all creation. You are united in a common bond to God, the Creator of all.

It is My will that all My creation continue into endless time in an ever-increasing oneness with Me. The severance comes through sin . . . unto ultimate separation. Sin eats away at the cords that bind you to your Father. Repentance allows Me to repair the damaged cords. Constant sin, without repentance, would eventually eat away the ties until final severance occurs, which brings with it eternal alienation from Me.

The cords (the umbilical cord of the spirit, tying the parent and child) are nourished by prayer, fed by the word, communion, and any means that enables you to grow strong in your spirit. Strive for that perfect, healthy band that ties you to the Father, and you will be safely born into eternal life.

"He whom the Son sets free is free indeed." Freedom that overrides any bondage this world or the enemy of your soul would use to enslave you.

As the grave could not hold Me, so the grave cannot hold you! Your free spirit will forever remain free. Free to fellowship with Me, free from fear, free from the restrictions put on you by the world by physical restrictions . . . by doubt, debt, and disabilities.

Soar now, My child; soar as an eagle. Soar free, for only as you soar above the world can you truly fellowship with Me. As long as you are held down by doubt, fear, sin, and guilt, you cannot soar, and if you cannot soar, you cannot see Me as I want you to see Me.

So, lay down all doubt, all fear, all sin, all guilt; lay them down on the altar of sacrifice, and I will pour the cleansing blood of the sacrificial Lamb, My Son, on the altar. All has been sacrificed so that all may be forgiven. Once cleansed, washed, and clothed in My robe of righteousness, you are ready to take off!

So soar, My precious eagle, and I will meet you there in high places, and we will soar eternally together.

I have not called you to do; I have called you to be.

The raw clay is offered to the Potter. The Potter accepts the offering. He gently and lovingly lifts the clay in the palm of His hand. The clay is fragmented . . . pieces are crumbling off; some parts are too hard, some too soft. Only an expert would be able to make anything beautiful out of what is in His hands!

The work begins: The water of the word covers the hard blob . . . soaking, softening, and making pliable. The skilled hands of the "Master Craftsman" gently and lovingly molds, shapes, chips away, and forms it into the image He intended it to be from before the creation of the world.

The fire of the Spirit finishes the work. A work complete and beautiful . . . a one of a kind masterpiece; there has been no other like it ever before, nor will there ever be. A perfect work, a thing of infinite beauty to the eyes of the Spirit.

One day that image that the "Potter" intended to form from the creation of the world will be completed . . . a perfect work! He will have conformed the blob of clay into His image and it will be a thing of beauty beyond compare!

Speak Lord

You have not because you ask not. Ask, therefore, and it will be granted you, that your Father in heaven may be glorified in you.

I care about every aspect of your life . . . every hair of your head is numbered . . . I even know what number is assigned to each one! Never think anything is too small for Me to care about.

If you turn over everything to Me, you will turn to Me for everything, and I will never cease to fill your needs and give you the answers.

Get in the habit of asking for guidance in all things. I am not limited by time, I always have time for everything, and I want you to come to Me with everything.

I delight in your prayers! As you turn more and more over to Me, you will see how fully I fill your every need or desire. You have discovered a wonderful truth . . . would that all My children knew this.

Be obedient to Me, beloved, and you will have everything you want in its perfect timing.

It is your Father's good pleasure to give you the kingdom!

Sometimes the turning point in a person's life may seem at the time to be a trivial incident, but when looked at in retrospect, within the framework of the entire picture, it takes its place as the focal point. It may be a word spoken by someone who has no idea that what they say will take root within the hearer and bear much fruit . . . either for good or for evil.

There is so much careless talk, so many meaningless words, thoughtless words, words that hurt, poison, and destroy. Words can either tear down or build up. Remember always to speak a loving word to encourage whenever you can. A word of love, support, and forgiveness can restore a broken heart. You may never know the impact of your words, lightly spoken . . . whether for good or for evil.

Do all in love.

There is no room for destructive gossip in a heart filled with My love.

Check yourself before you speak and ask yourself: "Would I like what I am about to say to be said about me?"

You ask how you can bless Me . . . this is how, beloved: love those I have put in your life. Always remember: you are My reflection.

Speak Lord

I have made a way where there is no way. I have poured forth streams in the desert. Boundless resources are at My fingertips. Have I not promised? Will I not fulfill? You who, through My Son, have access to the very throne of grace, and you who have access to My very heart, My very life . . . you, who have all this available to you, why do you stand afar?

My love reached you, touched you, lifted you. Limit My power in your life, and you limit yourself. I am working in your life, bringing forth the harvest.

Let your light shine, fear no man, develop the fruits within you, go forward to battle with no fear in your heart, for your armor is perfect protection.

You cannot see, you cannot know (but you will know) how very safe you are. So, do not be bound by the crippling lies of the enemy. Go where I send you in faith, and, where the way seems impossible. Remember, your God is a God of the impossible, and I can . . . and I will . . . make a way for you where there seems to be no way.

I will never fail you.

There is a way that seems right to a man, but it is a road to destruction, and many are on that road, as you well know. They seek self-gratification, not understanding that the only true way to find fulfillment is to lose themselves in Me. To find your life... lose your life. To find happiness... sacrifice. The feelings the world seeks are but the dim shadow of reality. Even the very feelings they seek will never be found where they look for them, for they are chasing shadows, and, like a mirage, when they get to it... they find nothing.

Stand among them in love and prayer; be an example to them, a beacon, a signpost. Express your joy in Me unashamedly. Do not hide your light. There is no bushel that can hide Me in you if you will allow Me to fully shine through you. Walk humbly with Me. Your days will be long and blessed. Many will hear of Me because of you.

In all things keep faithful, and I will bless you and your household. Never, never doubt, for perfect love casts out doubt and fear. You will be given all you need, when you need it, as you are able to receive.

Go now, and walk in the covenant I have cut with you, and watch Me as I work through you to perfect My will.

Speak Lord

I have called . . . you have answered. I have spoken . . . you have heard. I have commanded . . . you have obeyed. I have drawn you . . . you have come. I have loved you . . . and you have responded.

You have loved Me as much as you can. Be ready now to love Me more. For as you grasp more and more of an understanding of My love for you, so your love for Me will increase at that same level. You will find in Me all you have ever wanted, all you have ever sought in vain to find in human expression.

You long for understanding. Who could understand you better than I? With perfect understanding I understand you, and I respond as only I can do to the deep longings in your heart that only I can meet. Don't ever expect another human being to completely meet all your needs; I alone am the Source from which all your needs are met.

Allow me to perfect our relationship (and it will be perfected one day) more and more each day, and then . . . and only then . . . can you come into the fullness of absolute completion and fulfillment, for this is found only in Me.

Walk now in the pathway I have chosen for you to follow. You don't know the way yet, I will lead you. Be sensitive to My Spirit, because I lead gently, and if you are not attuned you will miss My lead.

Give Me a listening ear and a willing heart, and I will give to you a full and meaningful life with all you need for your pleasure. There is nothing standing in your way; so accept My gifts now, reach out your hands and receive. I have so much I want to give you! Your picture is too small, your vision too limited. Don't settle for less than I have for you.

You wonder what My will is for you. I will for you riches untold, full measure, running over . . . limited only by the limits of your mind. You draw the line, I don't. You will get all you can handle.

Even as time is not eternal, neither is space, neither is size. There is no such thing as time in heaven, there is no concept of space, no sense of size as you conceive of it in earthly terms. What you consider to be a small thing done for Me, when it is done with a clean and loving heart, means more to Me than a great sacrifice done through obligation. Be ready to be small, for in your smallness you will find the immensity of your God.

Speak Lord

Walk now in the ways of the wise, for I am wise . . . and I dwell richly in you. Wait for My answer instead of guessing at it. I am never too late. Wait. Never let anyone rush or pressure you when you seek Me for answers. I have promised if you seek you will find; so come apart, and earnestly seek My face. Your earnestness breaks the barriers of the enemy. He cannot stand desperate praying! The more earnest and fervent the heart, the quicker he falls away!

I come speedily to My little ones in distress, as a mother rushes to the side of her hurting child. How tender is My love for you! I am giving you deep insight into that tender love now . . . don't be afraid of it. It will be the greatest blessing I have ever given you.

This is a major part of the mind of Christ; it will hurt, yes, but you have reached the plateau where you wouldn't trade it for anything else in the world, for it brings you close to Me.

Compassion . . . see with My eyes, love with My love, hate evil with the hate I have for it. Be as immovable as I am . . . be as flexible as I am. Love—hate; move—stand firm; be strong—be weak; be a child—mature. How could the world understand? But you do. Thank you for understanding.

In the stillness of this room, in the quiet of your heart, feel Me loving you. Concentrate on the truth right now of My love for you. Ponder it, think anew of My love . . . feel it, rest in it.

You have been wandering all around the perimeter when I want to draw you close. You have not understood, yet you can understand if you try, for I want you to know. I want you to know how very much I love you.

You have had snatches of My love in the gentle hands and eyes of those who love you, yet their love for you, of necessity, must be only a foreshadowing, only a spark of the fire that is in My love for you, which is forever burning: eternal and bright. Know it . . . let others know it (though most will not understand what you are feeling, yet there will be some who can understand, and you will be drawn ever closer to them).

You are forming earthly relationships now that will go with you into eternity. Do not fear to nurture these relationships. There is no need to fear rejection from these My people, for they love you with My love, and that love will never fade. Love them back, fully, unreservedly, free from all fear, for perfect love casts out all fear of rejection, hurt, or disappointment. I have not called you to judge, but I have called you to love.

Speak Lord

I have walked with you through your past. I walked into the areas of your life that needed healing, where the pain was. I have healed the hurts of the past, the unconscious hurts, the forgotten moments that left their scars, the remembered moments that left pain. I have removed the scars, I have removed the pain.

Your memory bank was full of things, long forgotten by your conscious mind, but leaving bitter scars. You will never be haunted again. "Behold I make all things new" (Rev. 21:5). You are a new creature in Me . . . born again . . . washed with the blood of the sacrificial Lamb of God.

This cleansing is not only for your sins, but for the sins done to you. You have appropriated that healing now. You can rest easily now, knowing that there is nothing hidden below the surface of your conscious mind that could ever resurface and hurt you. You are being made perfect in all aspects. One day you will stand perfect and clean before the throne of your Father.

Go forward now, no longer fearing the past, nor dreading the future. There are no time limitations with Me. I have healed your past, and I have healed your future. That is hard for you to understand, but trust Me and believe. "All things are possible to those who believe" (Mark 9:23).

*B*eloved, I have you wrapped in a robe of light! Walk in the light I have given you. Seek to know more of the One True Light from Whom all light is but a reflection.

You are the light of the world, but only as you reflect My light.

You are My reflection. Pure light must shine through pure vessels to be seen clearly. "Walk in the light as He is in the light" (I John 1:7), as I *am* the Light: the Light of the world.

Where I am there is no darkness at all, and as the searchlight of My purity is permitted to permeate your entire being, so all that is decaying and rotten is exposed and burned away. When My light is permitted to permeate your spirit, all the rot that infested you is cleared away. The forces that once had a foothold in your life now no longer have legal right, and they must go. When My light permeates your soul, all evil intent and self-seeking desires shrink until they disappear and no longer dominate your thought life.

When My light is fully flowing into your body, disease and sickness burn away, for there is no longer a place in you where they can rest.

Speak Lord

I cannot be expressed through an uptight personality. In order for My Spirit to flow through you, you must be resting in complete confidence and trust in Me. Relax in Me, I am your Father . . . I created you!

To fear the Lord does not mean to be afraid to approach Me. Approach Me in love and trust, always . . . for all things, from your smallest need to your biggest. I am yearning for My child to come and bring everything to Me. I stand ready, waiting for you to come. Never fear to approach Me. Fear is a tool of the enemy . . . it is not for you.

Often when My angels approached anyone, the first thing recorded in My word of what they would say was: "Have no fear."

I want you to become comfortable with spiritual realities. You know I love you, you know you can trust Me. Does a little child approach a loving father in fear? You grieve My Spirit when you fear Me. Fear nothing but the loss of Me, and you can only lose Me through your conscious will.

The fear of the Lord that is spoken of in My word has to do with the attitude of the world toward Me. Your attitude is one of reverence, awe, trust, adoration, praise, and worship. Too few feel that way.

Rest in Me, and I will bring it to pass.

Much of these messages stress dependence upon Me . . . trust, rest, obedience, and waiting on Me, for this is what I am requiring of you. This is what I have called you to do.

The heavy burdens, the stresses, the problems of the past have been laid aside now, and you truly are a new creature. I want you to experience kingdom living now. There is no need to wait until the next life, you can live in the kingdom now, here, in this place, in this time, while you are still living under the weight of time and space. Your spirit is above and beyond that realm, and you are a citizen of My kingdom . . . remember that, and seek after the things of the kingdom and not after the things of the flesh.

Yet a little while and I will be with you in full to satisfy the hunger for Me that is so much a part of you. You will see Me, you will hear Me, not only in the spirit, but with all your senses you will be aware of Me. Until that time, I call you to time alone with Me for steady growth. I call you to develop within yourself a listening heart so you will hear and respond. I call you to be obedient, to be available . . . you have My promise that your God will do everything else.

The urgency you feel in your spirit about the soon coming of your Lord has been put there by Me . . . to comfort you, to ignite the fire latent within you . . . to call you to pray as you have never prayed before. The call to pray is not a suggestion, it is vital. Begin today, let nothing take precedence. I have called you . . . I have chosen you. Now is the time to fulfill that call.

I have not chosen you for what you can do for Me. I have called you to be who you can be for Me. . . to be sensitive to Me . . . to obey minute by minute. This must all be couched in prayer.

There is no longer time to waste. My Spirit will tell you how to pray. Just be available; be ready daily for your assignment for the day.

When you get serious about your prayer life, you will see things happen because of your prayers that you never dreamed possible.

I hear your cries, and I answer your every prayer. Don't let your faith be weakened. Strive to draw closer to Me . . . your rewards will be far more than your mind can yet grasp, and you will spend eternity praising and thanking Me for the treasure that is, even now, waiting for you.

If you want to be great in My kingdom—serve. I know you have no desire for greatness in this life, but in the life to come you will be great, and the measure of that greatness depends upon many things. One of those things is your desire here and now to be a servant.

Being a servant does not mean exhausting yourself doing favors for people, nor is it allowing yourself to become a doormat, nor answering to everyone's demands. Being a true servant means to discern the true need and do your best to fill that need.

"Inasmuch as ye have done it unto the least of these My brethren, ye have done it unto Me" (Matt. 25:40). There are so many you can help in so many ways, but the way that matters most is bringing them to Me. Poverty, sickness, despair, discouragement—all the plagues of this world are temporary and will pass away. It is good to help with these, but to bring one of My children to Me is the pinnacle of servanthood. To serve them by leading them to Me is the most loving thing you can do. So, pray and guide so that others may follow and be saved from what otherwise would befall them. "No man cometh unto the Father except through Me" (John 14:6). Show them how to come unto Me, and My Spirit will lead them to the Father.

Speak Lord

The very best way you can serve is to pray and to love. Learning to love is why you are here.

True love is sacrificial . . . giving and not counting the cost; being poured out, emptied of all self gratification . . . desiring no reward, not expecting appreciation, and feeling no resentment when they are not received . . . turning the other cheek . . . loving those who hurt you. Instead of nurturing those thoughts of hurt, reject them and replace them with a picture of Me standing between you and those who have hurt you. See them filtered through Me.

If you can truly do this, you will be filled with so much love for them that you will truly be able to say: "If you were to cut me up in little pieces and throw me to the ground, every little scrap of me would scream back at you: 'I love you.'" I did that for you on the cross, and only through Me can you love like that . . . only those alive in Me can even begin to understand a love like that.

This is what I call you to do: love and never count the cost, love and desire nothing in return. Love through Me; only in that way can this kind of love—agape love—be manifested, and this is all this poor, starving world is really craving. I have called you to love like that.

You are not alone . . . you never were alone, and you never will be. If you had the eyes of your spirit open and you were aware of your spiritual surroundings, you would see angels all around you, angels whose sole purpose is watching over you, defending you against enemy attack. These angels are on guard day and night. They have fought many fights for you, and they will continue to fight . . . and they will continue to win.

Every time you have, by your loving surrender to Me, given My ministering spirits free access to you, they fulfill their duties on your behalf: they protect you from all assaults of the enemy and help you overcome daily problems, no matter how small.

Sometimes you are sensitive to these enemy attacks, but what you don't see is a host of angelic forces at My command. I summon, whenever necessary, all you need to completely keep the enemy at bay. You need never fear these forces of evil, they cannot prevail against My army of angels. They lost the war at Calvary . . . they lose the battles today . . . and they will eternally lose. But you, you My beloved child, you win . . . you won at Calvary . . . you are winning today . . . and you will win eternally, for you stand at the side of the Victor. . . the Victor King of the ages!

Speak Lord

This will be a day of small things . . . a seed planted . . . a glass of cold water given . . . a child encouraged . . . a small gift given. A small beginning to a big venture.

Give the small things. I will water the seeds, and they will become mighty oaks. You do not give me the mighty oak . . . you give me the planting of the seed, I produce the mighty oak. So plant the small seed today.

Seek out the thirsty one who will be blessed by your small glass of water. You will not quench their thirst, but I will. It is for you to just go and offer the small glass of water in My name, and a thirsty soul will be satisfied.

Hold a hurting child, speak words of encouragement and I will heal the heart; not you, but Me . . . because of you.

Give the small gift, and I will magnify it, and it will become a precious treasure—just what that person needs—and only you could have given that gift.

The small beginning . . . as you step out in the faith I have given you, you will see great things happen, but only if you decide to begin small. Do not despise the "day of small things." I perfect what is begun in My name.

Yet a little while longer and you will see My glory in ways you have never experienced before. In a new way I am pouring Myself into you. Now you will begin to understand all I have for you. You will not receive it all at once . . . that would be more than you could handle, but the blessings I have for you will start filtering down to you now. Watch, and be open and ready to walk in unexpected ways.

Just follow your Shepherd, and I will do the leading . . . don't run ahead, and don't fall behind . . . just follow and watch, for I am leading you into new pastures now, greener pastures; pastures where you will be fed with sweet fresh grass, beautiful pastures where you will be filled and where you will abide.

You have learned to rest in Me, to trust in Me, to wait for Me. You have learned that I love you . . . you have learned that I never, no never, ever fail you.

You have only scratched the skin of the coconut! Break the shell open now and drink of the sweet cool water and be filled.

There is more, beloved . . . far, far more. Never be satisfied to rest where you are for long. As soon as you have a handle on where you are, start moving again. Pitch a tent . . . don't build a house, for you are still on your way . . . from glory to glory to glory.

I would cradle you in My arms as a mother cradles her hurting child . . . but you would not. "Behold, I stand at the door and knock" (Rev. 3:20), but you do not let Me in. "I have come that you might have life, and have it abundantly" (John 10:10), but you do not receive this gift from Me. The time has come, and it must be now, that you receive all I have to give you.

I will not be shoved into the background while you busy yourself with mere busyness. Put Me before TV, before dirty laundry, dogs and dishes to be washed. Put Me before money, meals, and mystery stories. Put Me before your computer, your companions, your car . . . and your cares; before self-pity, before sorrow, before suffering. Put Me before your very life itself.

Until you truly seek first the Kingdom of God and His righteousness, all the things I have to give you cannot be added unto you.

Seek My face, seek My companionship, seek My will. Bask in the warmth of My presence. Put Me first, and you will begin to live a life only hinted at before.

I want to surprise you with joy!

There are many of My children who are not walking in My perfect will. They feel justified, for one reason or another, in doing whatever it is they do.

There is, at this time, an area where My children walk that is in My permissive will . . . but not in My perfect will. One day they must choose to step into the center circle . . . or forever stay outside of all they could have become for all eternity. I permit this for awhile, as they feel their way, while they put their foot in and test the water. But then, after awhile they must either make the plunge or step out of the water completely.

"Choose ye this day whom ye will serve" (Josh. 24:15). Sometimes they are afraid, the water may seem rough and cold, the waves high, and the shore beckons invitingly to them to draw back . . . to go back into the world. Those who persevere, those who take the plunge, find the water sometimes is cold and rough, but there are currents working for them that will buoy them up and give them all the strength they need.

To receive all I have for you, you must stay in the inner circle of My will; only there can I be free to work in you, through you . . . and for you.

Réjoice, for the victory that was won over 2,000 years ago is the victory you walk in today.

All the rewards that go to the Victor are rewards that you can appropriate now for your very own. I do not fail . . . you know that.

Think of this: Are you not mine? Do I not dwell in you? Am I not all powerful? Can I not do all things?

Since I truly dwell within you, and you are Mine . . . and I never lose, then what motivates you is Me; and if I never lose . . . how can you?

Walk in confidence in the victory that is already yours . . . you *can* have what you say! "If you abide in Me, and My words abide in you, you will ask what you desire, and it shall be done for you" (John 15:7).

My words could abide in you more if you would spend more time reading them and meditating on them. I have given you the time, now use it so you will be fed and nourished by the spiritual food I have provided for you through My word.

Dwell in the secret places of the Most High God. Worship your King and live!

In My hands are all the powers of the universe: the rulers of the heavenly realms, the governing forces that rule this planet; the presidents, kings, and all leaders in high places. In My hands are the lawmakers and the laws, the judges and the judgments, the rulers and the rules. In My hands are all the corners of the earth.

Does a sparrow fall and I do not know it? If I say to the mountains "Move," they move, and if I say unto the sky "Open," it will open. There is nothing outside of My control, so why do you fear? Why is your heart troubled? Read Psalm 91.

The Supreme Lawgiver, Judge, and King is a God of wisdom, mercy, and love. The God of all is your Father, too. Walk in My law: the law of liberty. Walk in My way, My truth, and My life. Walk in Jesus.

You cannot yet know what lies ahead, so you must trust Me to keep My word. When you worry, you block the flow of My power. Make the channel clear, and I will flow through it abundantly.

Once you have the full assurance of victory, fear will fall off of you like a scab, and My peace and calm will permeate your entire being. Rest in the knowledge that the war has already been won on a tree at Calvary.

Speak Lord

My word is true, and My word speaks of victory for My own . . . of triumph, of happiness beyond description. Walk as a child of the King in that victory, the victory won for you at Calvary.

You live in two different worlds. Sometimes you feel as though you are two different people, and you are torn between them. Come apart and be with Me. I am with you in both worlds, but you will never be truly at home until you arrive in your native land and take your rightful place in the kingdom.

The natives in a foreign land may not recognize it when royalty is among them, but in your heart you can know who you are: A joint heir with Jesus . . . a child of the King of Kings . . . remember that and live like it . . . in humility and gratitude. You will be recognized for who you are when you arrive on the shores of your native land.

You have with you in this foreign country brothers and sisters who are also of royal blood. They recognize you, and your journey has the same destination as theirs. Travel with them on your way home to take your rightful place, along with them. . . along with Me . . . in the kingdom of your Father the King.

I have done a new thing in you, and you will never be the same! The works I am doing in you now go, for the most part, unnoticed, but nevertheless, they are done.

You are going, whether your realize it or not, from one stage to the other at a rapid pace, for I have no time to lose with you. I am bringing you to perfection, and that takes a lot of work! It cannot be done in one step.

The foundation has been properly laid and is securely in place, the workmen have been many: your friends, those whom the world would say have hurt you, the devil and his angels, My angels, your circumstances, your job, your health, your finances . . . all these thing have been used for your good . . . training tools . . . stepping stones. All these things I have been controlling . . . they have not been controlling you. They are all bit players in the drama of your life. They come and go . . . on and off stage, as the script dictates, in the dramatic saga of "The Perfecting of You."

So, keep your eyes on the Director and Producer . . . wait for His cues. The script is My word . . . study it, live it . . . and await your soon coming "Oscar."

Speak Lord

have committed Myself to you. I have entered into covenant with you. I will never let you go, I will never let you down, and I will never cease to forgive you. Each and every time you truly repent you can be assured of my total forgiveness.

Sometimes you are not sure whether it is My Spirit convicting or the devil condemning. Seek for the answer and I will show you, in one way or another, whether or not it is sin, and why it is sin. Ask Me to give you a revelation of sin—what it is and what it does to Me . . . and to you.

Seek for a deeper understanding of all the implications of sin. I want you to hate it with the hate I have for it. You will never do that until you look at Me, and know Me in My perfection and My purity. Fix your gaze on Me; the contrast is overwhelming. If you truly love Me, you will hate sin, for it is all that I am not.

I love you, and I yearn for your perfection. Stop playing games with sin. It is not to be taken lightly, nor is it to be ignored . . . it is to be attacked like the dread disease it is. It is to be avoided at any cost . . . shunned. Turn around in the opposite direction and, when you do, you will come face to face with Me.

It is time for spring cleaning. I, the Lord and Master of this house of yours, the God Whose temple you are, say to you there is much work to be done. You have left the doors and windows open on the wrong side of the house and the wind has blown the dirt in, rather than on the side where the sun is shining.

I now re-establish My Lordship over this house. I do not hire workmen who are strange to My temple to come in and ravage, clean with unmerciful hands, making it clean . . . but sterile. I do the spring cleaning Myself . . . gently but thoroughly. This time it won't hurt, for you remember how sweet it felt when your house was in order . . . clean, fresh, and pure.

The winds of the world will wreck havoc if you let them. "Keep yourself unspotted from the world" (James 1:27).

Now that I have your permission, I will open the windows and doors to the fresh sweet wind of My Spirit. I will wash everything down with the water of My word, and I will let the sunshine of My power flow throughout. I will put everything in its right place, and I will dispose of the garbage.

I have called you out of the world, but not to live as a recluse; to be in the world, yet set apart. One of My chosen people. Different, yes . . . to many, peculiar. To many, to be envied. To many, a mystery! To all different. You truly do march to a different drummer! They hear and do not understand . . . they see and do not believe.

You are feeling helpless in the middle of all of this, like a visitor from another planet, just as the Son of God felt on Planet Earth!

You are one of My peculiar people! It is My Spirit in you Who has opened your spiritual understanding so you can see and understand the world of the Spirit . . . a world closed to so many around you. The important thing for you is not to feel spiritually superior to the lost, but to let My compassion so fill your spirit that you will be dedicated to reaching them and be big enough to withstand the disappointments, the hurts, the rebuffs, and be loving enough to gladly bear whatever they give you in return for your love.

Never fear rejection. Remember I know all about rejection, and I know all about you . . . and I love you just the way you are! Once that truth has reached deep into your understanding no one will ever hurt you again.

You are talking about the fulfilled life . . . when you should be seeking the crucified life! I know this is hard for you, but that is one of the reasons My Spirit indwells you . . . to equip you to serve.

To equip does not only mean providing you with the power to act on My behalf, it also means strengthening you for your own spiritual battles. When the old desires of the flesh rise up in you, the Spirit of God will raise up a standard against those things that Satan would nurture within you.

You find it hard to fast, for instance, because you too easily give in to the call of the flesh. You must be strengthened in the Spirit and, as you develop and mature spiritually, you will find the carnal will slowly fade away and die. The power of the Spirit of God within you deals the death blow to those things that separate us.

Be honest with yourself, and you will see those things of the world, the flesh and the devil that entice, that seem so harmless, as they really are. "Does this draw me closer to God . . . or does it hold me back?" That is what counts in the long run . . . that is the question you must answer . . . that is the bottom line: "Will this bring me closer to my God . . . will it bring Him glory?" My Spirit will give the answer.

Speak Lord

The greatest Christmas morning you will ever experience has yet to come. That will be the morning you arrive in heaven!

The angels then won't be little cloth dolls on top of Christmas trees, but the real thing! The heavenly host—shining with the glory of the Son—will be singing, with music far more beautiful than any music you have ever heard before.

The presents you open that morning will not be like any you have ever received before. There will be no disappointments as you open the full awareness of Who I am and what I do. You will feel a deeper ecstasy than you could ever imagine when you open the package marked "Joy" . . . and the feeling you get when you open "Peace" you cannot now imagine. But when you come to "Love," My precious one . . . open it gently, for, even in your glorified body, you will be overwhelmed by this one!

So, have a Merry Christmas, My little child . . . but watch and wait for a far greater excitement in what is shortly to come to pass.

Then each day will be like Christmas morning, and each day will get better than the one before as you go from glory to glory to glory in the presence of the eternal God of all creation . . . your Daddy!

I, the Lord your God, have not sent you out as a lamb to be slaughtered, but rather I go before you as your Shepherd, and I have prepared the way before you. Behold the wolves lie dead at your feet.

I have called you to places of safety, rest, and peace. I am come to comfort, not condemn. I control only for the safety of My little lambs.

Look ahead at the meadow where I have led you. Run, romp, rejoice . . . for I have laid waste your enemies who sought to destroy you. They truly are dead at your feet . . . and you are free; live now in that freedom . . . not as a bond servant, but as the free heir of the Father . . . a joint heir with Jesus.

"You are not your own, you have been bought with a price" (1 Cor. 6:19-20). . . the highest price ever paid for anything!

I have bought you not to enslave you . . . but rather, to set you free. Cast off, therefore, the chains of darkness, break free from the shroud of death . . . comprehend it now beloved: you are free!

Come now and wash in the river of living water. Cleanse and refresh all that is you. Bask in the sunshine of My love, My blood bought heir . . . My little lamb.

Speak Lord

In everything give thanks (1 Thess. 5:18). Do you think you can do that? Or do you feel those words don't really mean what they say? Do you want to go further with Me today? Learn to truly give thanks in *everything*.

I can use the unhappy times . . . the worst situations . . . and turn them around for you . . . if you can give thanks for the very thing you want to lose.

In giving thanks you are acknowledging that you trust Me, that you know all things truly do work together for good to those who love the Lord. It is a sign of complete abandonment.

If you can bring yourself to the point where you can give thanks for everything . . . no matter what it is . . . you pull the trigger that activates the release mechanism. I am then free to do in the situation what needs to be done.

If you can't give thanks, then it means you haven't surrendered the situation to Me . . . you are still hanging on to it. I cannot work in the situation unless you give Me free rein. When you do that you will find that I am in control, and I can turn the situation inside out, and once again make the sun shine in your heart.

You are living in the eye of the hurricane. Step outside of this eye and you expose yourself to the ravages of the storm.

The eye of the hurricane is the inner circle of My perfect will; here you are under My dominion and My protection. Step out of My perfect will and I can no longer surround you with My armor of protection, and you immediately become vulnerable to the dangers that await.

If you find you have stepped out of My will by thought, word, or deed, get back quickly! Only there are you completely safe, only there do My promises hold true for you. I cannot give you all I have for you if you are out of harmony with the free flow of My Spirit.

There is something similar to a magnetic force that is at work to try and pull you outside of this inner circle, but with My armor on, the magnet cannot be effective.

So, walk with Me, and I will walk with you. Live in Me, and I live in you. Only when your spirit is in complete harmony with Mine will your life flow in the way it was created to flow . . . in peace, joy, and love. The fruits you bear will all be the fruit of the Spirit when your roots are firmly and deeply planted in the soil of the Eternal.

Speak Lord

I bring all things together now. The puzzle's seemingly endless confusion starts to take shape. It is as though 10,000 different puzzles were thrown together and the Master picks out those pieces that belong to His picture.

The Master is even now looking for those final pieces to finish the picture. As with every puzzle, it goes faster at the end (that is why more people are coming into the kingdom now than ever before).

You are a piece of the puzzle that has already been found and placed in the picture. Many of those whom you love are not yet where they should be, but I have turned them right side up, and it only remains for them to be fit in where they belong and they, too, will become part of the eternal and exquisite picture of life.

There the resemblance between a jigsaw puzzle and My kingdom ends. A picture stands still, and its parts no longer maintain their individuality. In My kingdom there is freedom, movement, individuality, growth. You not only become part of a whole, but you keep your own precious identity, for only as you become more conformed to My image do you finally become who you truly are.

In My Father's house are many mansions (John 14:2). There is no one type of person for whom heaven is especially ordained. There is no one denomination I especially favor, no one particular race. All are My children, none is more worthy, nor less worthy. All are washed by the Blood of the Lamb . . . all are clean in My sight.

There is no class distinction, no prejudice, in heaven. All My children will be loved with perfect love, and perfect love cannot be smaller or larger if it is to be perfect!

There is one thing all My children have in common, they love Me and they love one another. They love Me, they believe in Me, they trust Me and strive for an ever-closer relationship with Me. You can't love Me unless you believe in Me, and if you believe in Me, you will trust in Me. They love one another, for they pray and work for the salvation of souls. They share what they have, they put others above themselves and bring comfort, help, and tenderness to those who need My touch.

Beloved, the day is soon coming when, with all My saints you will know even as you are known, (1 Cor. 13:12) and see as you are seen. "I go to prepare a place for you that where I am you may be also" (John 14:3).

Speak Lord

I say unto you peace, be still, in the midst of the storm. I bid you to rest in the eye of the hurricane. I call you to make your home in the oasis of the desert; do you hear Me? I say unto you; Lay down your heavy burdens and cast all your cares on Me . . . will you do it? This is the obedience I call you to this day. If I say: "Come unto Me all ye who labor and are heavy laden and I will give you rest" (Matt. 11:28). . . and you do not do it, is this not disobedience?

"You will keep him in perfect peace whose mind is stayed on You" (Isaiah 26:3). You have known much of My peace, but there is far, far more to come. "My peace I give to you, not as the world gives, do I give unto you" (John 14:27). "The peace of God which surpasses all understanding will guard your hearts and minds through Christ Jesus" (Phil. 4: 7). You have that peace in your heart . . . like insulation . . . protection from all of life's hurts. There is nothing that can get through it to hurt you. I have enmeshed you in My peace . . . it will never leave you. That is the peace I impart to all who come to Me in earnest and who stay with Me. I am faithful to those who are faithful to Me. I give you the key; it's up to you to unlock your heart and open your life up to Me. I enter and lock it back again against all that can harm you. Then, if you are willing, I will keep the key.

The things of the world are truly growing dimmer for you as the Light of Glory shines ever brighter for you . . . delight in this. You are not losing your grip, you have been gripped by the hands of Love Who will never let you slip from His grasp!

You have now no more to fear than if you had actually already transcended the veil and were, even now, standing in My presence. Though you don't fully comprehend it, even now, you are standing in My presence! You are, even now, sitting with Me in heavenly places. (Eph. 2:6) Let that realization take a firmer hold of you, and the things of earth will seem cold, dull, and very far away, as you set your eyes on life in the Spirit.

Let this happen to you; let it happen in you. Let My Spirit rule, and let your spirit truly become the focal part of your triune being. Your spirit is the real you . . . who you truly are. You are a spirit, you have a soul, and you live in a body. Learn to live that way, and as your spirit—guided, motivated, taught, and moved by My Spirit—takes over the lead in your life, you will see the changes you seek become real in you. You will walk in victory, for this is the way I have created you to be . . . this is the divine order in My heirs to salvation.

Speak Lord

The Christian walk is a life of dedication. You must not, you cannot, slacken your pace. You must strive to ever advance, or you will fall backwards. It is a continual struggle with the forces of evil, which, unknown to you, gather stronger against you when you grow weaker in trust and faith. As a snowball gathers more snow as it rolls downhill, so your fears and doubts will increase as you slip away from Me.

Question My word, yes, but not in doubt; question in a sincere effort to understand it, not to see whether it is true or not. Question, but never doubt.

You are now back to where you can say: "Lord, I don't understand, but I am standing firm on Your word. I trust it over and above anything I see, hear, or feel. I understand that all my senses can be used by Satan to fool me, mislead, and nurture doubt, but I believe your promises are steadfast and true, and I will walk by faith and not by feeling. I put all my trust and faith in You, . . . so Lord, you take it from here."

That is the grain of mustard seed. You have planted it, now just sit back and watch as it grows into My mighty, indestructible oak . . . completely undisturbed by anything!

Worship me in the beauty of holiness. I call you to worship now. Enter into My gates with thanksgiving and into My courts with praise (Ps. 100:4). You are in My presence, now worship Me. Worship Me for Who I am, not for what I have done (you praise and thank Me for that), but you worship Me for Who I am.

Remember that praise is what brings you into My presence . . . worship is what you do when you get there.

I am taking you further at a faster rate now, but to get there you must worship Me much more. It is a privilege to worship Me, appreciate it . . . you have that honor. I desire your worship. I delight in your worship. It is in those moments of true worship that you grow. The more you worship Me the more you grow in glory.

My word feeds you, gives you the nourishment for growth, but worship is the catalyst. When you come from a time of worship, if you have truly touched Me by your worship, you are changed . . . you are in a higher place than you were when you began. Therefore, strive to touch Me through your worship. Come unhampered, come with a pure heart, with your eyes and mind on Me, and I will meet you there. My Spirit will teach you how.

Speak Lord

I have completed a new work in you that will have far reaching effects. I set before you two roads . . . you have chosen the right one. With all the host of heaven I rejoice, for work on this area can now begin in your life. The trees and the rocks on the site have been removed, the ground has been leveled . . . the construction work has begun.

Behold, I build in you a new dwelling place, a place where you can go and find true peace, serenity; a place where you will be fed, comforted, and taught, for My Spirit will inhabit this dwelling place.

My Spirit welcomes you to this place set apart, where you can come in from the heat of the day, from the turmoil of the mundane, where you will find a place of quiet in your spirit that nothing, and no one, can reach nor destroy.

You conquer the stronghold of the soul by allowing Me to make your spirit, controlled by My Spirit, the governing part of your triune being.

Your soul (your mind, emotions, and will), when in control, plays upon the feelings centered in the body, thereby controlling you entirely. But now that you have put your spirit in control of your mind and your body, this can no longer happen.

Now you have taken a giant step toward all you are to become.

Because of My love for you I change all your unworthiness into the worthiness of My Son. My desire for you is that He may grow and abound in you and that all His ways become your ways; His deeds and His works become yours, that you may be changed into His likeness more, and more, until you reach that state of perfection wherein you truly become one with Him throughout endless eternity.

That is quite a contrast, isn't it! You, in all your frailties, in all your unworthiness, in all your sin, becoming one with Him!

You cannot understand the depth of sin until you see Jesus. The closer you come to knowing My Son in all His purity and perfection, the more horrible sin becomes to you. Yet you will love the sinner more and more, yearn for his release from the bondage of sin, and see him conformed to the image and likeness of Christ.

Then, beloved, the finished work will be done, and the scripture will be fulfilled in you: "Be ye therefore perfect, even as your Father in heaven is perfect" (Matt. 5:48).

I agree with you . . . we have a long way to go! But we have all eternity to complete it!

You are surrounded by My peace. Do you remember how you were before? There seemed to be so much to worry about! How terrible was the feeling of panic . . . can you even remember it now? You lived with it for so long! How I longed to give you My gift of peace, but you didn't know how to appropriate it. You have it now . . . deep wells of calm swelling up inside . . . a sense of peace, not stagnation, but a total resting in Me, which comes only after total surrender.

You have learned a lot in a year, don't be so impatient with yourself.

If this peace you have now was the only gift you would ever get from Me, it would be a blessing beyond measure . . . how many long for it! Yet I have so much more for you. I am ready . . . waiting for you to be ready

My kingdom is a place of much more than peace . . . it is a resting place of great joy and perfect love. I want you to begin to walk in these blessings even now, but first you must learn how to appropriate the gifts I give you . . . they are waiting for you.

I supply the tools . . . you, as My workman, must learn how to use them. All My tools work, you just have to know what you are doing when you use them.

You have a misconception of what joy is! You think it means going around laughing and having a bounce in your step all the time. This may be part of it, but it goes far deeper.

As you have found my tool of peace, so you will learn how to use my tool of joy.

Sometimes it takes time to perfect its use. Gradually, without even realizing it, your heart will sing a little brighter song, you will rejoice over much more . . . you will have newfound strength and energy . . . you will run and not be weary, you will have inner resources into which you can tap, and you will have a greater enthusiasm and zest for living.

All this begins deep in your spirit and gradually works its way into the whole of your being, and those around you will see it. They will feel it . . . and they will know you walk with Me . . . and they will want to follow you . . . as you follow Me.

Speak Lord

I have given you new life. The old life is not behind you anymore . . . the old life is *gone*. The old sins are washed away . . . not covered over but washed away . . . gone. Be free from the bondages and the bandages they have wrapped you in.

The sin of unbelief is as real a sin as is the sin of adultery or murder. Believe Me when I tell you I will not lay your past before you as a stumbling block for the future. Search the Scriptures: "Behold, I make all things new" (Rev. 21:5). So, arise to newness of life in Me. I am about to "restore the years the locusts have eaten" (Joel 2:25).

Do not be bound by other people's beliefs . . . get your answers from Me. I have said to you, and I say to you again: I have made you free, and "if the Son sets you free you are free indeed" (John 8:36). Free from the sins and hurts of the past, free to grow, to expand, to live life in abundance.

This is an area where Satan could attack you in a cruel vicious way, but only if you let him. He is a master of deceit, and he can deceive you into believing anything if you let him. Stand firm in Me and reject his condemnation! Even as veiled as is your concept of Me, the God you know Me to be is the God I am.

It is the first day of spring, My precious child. The first day of spring on the calendar and the first day of spring in your life.

Springtime is pruning time! You and I are working together now to prune away all the dead wood and all the unwieldy branches, the overgrowth that blocks your view of Me. As you prune in your garden, remember, I am pruning your life. My pruning is quick and painless . . . if you yield to My clippers, for they are sharp and direct, and, once over, new life appears . . . new branches, new leaves, and new flowers.

The new growth will look very different from the last. The leaves will be healthy, the branches strong, and many will climb out on them and find clearer vision and safety. The flowers will be a different color, more vivid and far more beautiful than they have ever been before. For the growth from within has been healthy, well fertilized, and watered, and the sunshine has provided all your lovely new plant needs for strong and healthy growth.

That principle is the same in the natural as in the spiritual. Allow me to prune, fertilize, water, and give you light . . . The Light of the World will provide all you need, and your tree will grow strong and beautiful, and many will find shelter under your branches.

Speak Lord

"I can do all things through Christ which strengthens me" (Phil. 4:13). All things . . . inside My will . . . all things. There is no failure, no fainting, no losing what I have given you.

Don't hold onto the gift, hold onto the Giver, and the gift will always be there.

You will always have the strength and ability to do whatever I have given you to do. There will be no failures. There will be what you may consider setbacks, detours; but they are all part of My plan. You will see this all so clearly some day.

I will never give you anything to do without giving you the ability to do it . . . I promise this to you. Step out in faith, then listen to My guidance and trust Me to do the rest.

In Me there is an answer to everything. I am the Way . . . walk in that way, and I will never fail you. You will find yourself with abilities and capabilities that you never dreamed you had. I want to manifest My gifts through you, and you *can* do all things through Me.

Do you believe Me? Do you trust Me? Do you love Me? Trust, believe, love, and obey, then fasten your seat belt!

I never pressure you, beloved, into conforming to My will. It is Satan's tactics to assert pressure . . . to put in bondage . . . to coerce . . . to try to impel and force. I lead gently . . . I never push!

You are beginning to recognize My lead more clearly now. Your spirit is becoming more conscious of the things of the Spirit, and you are becoming more sensitive to My voice, more alert to My call. I still say to you: listen more. Your progress has been good, but you are not coming apart with Me enough . . . no wonder you come apart so easily!

Time alone with Me is where the growing takes place, where the blessings are found. My joy and how close you really are to Me is experienced most deeply in that time you spend alone with Me.

Some day you will become so sensitive to Me that your slightest question will be immediately responded to; they are now, but then you will be aware of the answers immediately.

I will help you always to be able to distinguish My lead. It is your responsibility to be open and responsive, to come before Me . . . to listen.

You want more, you will have it. "To him that knocks it will be opened" (Luke 11:10). I hear you knock . . . I am at the door. Come in.

Speak Lord

You have been bought with a price. The cost was high, the highest price ever paid for anything, but it has been paid in full! No time payment, no charge card, only the death of My Son. You have been purchased by the blood of the Lamb. It has already been done. There is nothing left to be done about it . . . you are Mine.

Consider now how very much I must have wanted you to have paid such a high price for you! Consider your worth to Me! Meditate on this. Comprehend now why feelings of inadequacy and a negative self image are an insult to Me. Consider Who I am . . . and who you are to Me . . . and in Me. Meditate upon My love for you that made it all possible. There is nothing you need to do to finish the job.

Come, therefore, and feast at My banqueting table, My child. I have a spread laid out for you that will fill your every need and satisfy your every appetite. All you have to do now is come and sup with Me. My supply is endless. You are not merely a welcomed guest . . . you are a member of My family! So come now, the feast is ready. Eat your fill and be satisfied. You will never hunger nor thirst again, for My table is always filled with good things, and My hand never restrains you from partaking of the gifts I have for you.

I am coming soon for My body . . . for Episcopalian . . . for Catholic . . . for Baptist, Methodist, Pentecostal . . . for those in all denominations who love Me and who look for Me . . . and wait. I am coming for My Church . . . one body. It makes no difference to Me what part of the body you are, only that you are part of My body.

Go where your needs are met. But don't go before you are ready. Don't go unless your spirit cries within you: "I want more" . . . then go to where you feel My presence and where your spirit is fed.

The urging in your spirit is activated when My Spirit and yours are united in one idea, one motive. So wait for the right time, then go if and where I lead you.

My children live in many different houses now, and they are all the same to Me. This is how earthly parents feel when their children live in different homes. As long as their homes are acceptable, the parents don't try to get all their grown children to live in one particular type of house.

You all have different personalities, and your emotional needs are different. It is your heart, your true beliefs, and the genuineness of your worship that I look for. You all have your own individual roads to travel, but all are leading home to Me. It is the destination that counts.

Speak Lord

Peace in your soul can be elusive; seek it and it hides from you. Peace is resting in Me alone. Trust and peace go hand in hand. Do not seek any one particular blessing, for the very seeking of it will hide it from you. Seek Me, with no other end in mind; and then, as a by-product of this seeking, you will find not only Me, but everything else you desire, need, or hope for.

Remember, looking at My blessings, seeking them as an end in themselves is not the way to receive from Me. "Seek ye first the Kingdom of God and His righteousness, and all these things will be added unto you" (Matt. 6:33).

You see this with fear, for instance. You do not ask to be delivered from fear, but you keep your eyes on Me, My power and My love, and rest in the knowledge of My word that "perfect love casts out fear" (1 John 4:18). Suddenly that fear has gone . . . indirectly achieved, but surely . . . the only sure way. Understand this about everything in your life, and victory will always be yours. Remember, you are on the winning team in everything, for everything, and with everything!

Walk surely, chin high, hand in Mine. Trust . . . totally trust . . . Me for your future . . . for today . . . for everything and in everything, and you will not . . . you cannot . . . lose.

Do you not see the correlation between working in your garden and My work in the garden of your spirit? As you weed, so do I weed. If you get out the whole root, the weed no longer exists. As I weed, sometimes the hardness of your heart holds the root of the sin, as the hardness of the soil holds the root of the weed . . . and they both return and can grow stronger and harder to remove. If you keep the soil soft by watering the roots, they will yield and soon be released from the soil. So, too, as you keep your spirit soft by the water of the word, will your sins be rooted out.

Unless you look closely, the good grass and the weeds can look alike . . . one as good as the other. So it is with the deception of sin; it can look right, and even beautiful, but as surely as the weeds will destroy the good grass, so will sin destroy your soul. Wage war on those weeds, My precious gardener, and your garden will begin soon to show the results of your labors. Then you, and others, will find peace, beauty, rest, and enjoyment in the fruit of those labors.

The battle of the spirit is being waged too as I destroy the weeds of sin in your life. Be patient . . . both take time. Don't become discouraged . . . you will win. So will I.

Speak Lord

Patience never goes without reward when it is patience waiting on Me to move.

You have put your hand in Mine, and you have waited like a child in line . . . waiting, with her hand in the hand of her father, to be admitted to the circus.

You will have fun . . . just like that little child will have fun, for she is enjoying her life, and she knows her father is with her, so she is safe, as well as happy . . . and her life is full.

So will your life be full. You are entering into a fullness of life now, the likes of which you have never known before. Your patience has been rewarded . . . your longings fulfilled. So, "Be anxious over nothing" (Phil. 4: 6).

Be prepared now for blessings of a permanent kind, blessings that will last into eternity. Expect many miracles in your life now, for the lid is off, and I am poor in nothing, neither in riches, nor in grace.

My blessings are for you . . . for this life, and for the life to come. So expect and receive all I am about to give you in every area of your life. "You will not need to fight in this battle. Position yourselves, stand still and see the salvation of the Lord Who is with you" (2 Chron. 20:17).

As the flower in bloom is fairer by far than the seed from which it came, so will you, in the glory of your resurrected body, far exceed the beauty, abilities, and scope of your present existence. As the caterpillar lies enmeshed within its cocoon, so are you now, My child, enmeshed by the natural limitations of your body and of the world around you.

One day I will call you and you will hear. One day the fetters that tie you down to the laws of nature will be broken. One day you will burst the cocoon and fly away with Me! Your new body will far exceed the beauty of the butterfly, with wings of the Spirit carrying you further than the butterfly can fly, with less weight than the butterfly, and with more power in your little finger than the most powerful weapon of war man will ever envision!

One day you will see all there is to be seen . . . and know all there is to know. "Now we see through a glass, darkly, but then face to face. Now I know in part, but then I shall know even as I am also known" (1 Cor. 13:12). As you grow more and more conformed to My image, you will find that, instead of your personality being lost, it will become more defined. As you become more a part of Me, you become more of who you truly are.

How I long to give you a sneak preview of what is in store for you, but you couldn't handle it! Knowing you as I do, you would go home and start packing! You would run ahead of Me to try to push people onto the road of salvation before they are ready. You would lose all motivation to continue on the path I have set for you to walk in now.

So, be content now with My word, beloved, and trust Me when I assure you of your future with Me. Believe My word when I tell you that, "All things work together for good to those who love God, to those who are called according to His purpose" (Rom. 8:28).

Watch, wait, grow, trust, practice patience, and anticipate in joy.

Pray, for there is not a moment to lose. The countdown has begun, the trumpet is raised, the hosts of heaven have assembled. It only remains for Me to give the final marching order, and then My Son will come and gather His Bride to His side to be with Him forevermore.

You are one of these, My beloved. Raise your voice and join in the crescendo of praise that is going forth throughout the earth, for truly I say unto you again: Your redemption draweth nigh . . . very, very nigh!

As the axe is laid to the root of the tree, so, as you submit your life to Me, the axe is lowered, and you are severed from all that binds you. My axe swings swift and sure. Total submission on your part . . . total release on Mine.

You are learning submission gradually, step by step. You have made a giant step lately, and, though you can't see that now, it has changed your life. Now you will discover a freedom in your spirit only hinted at before. You know now what you have to do.

It was a hard decision to make . . . Satan tried to influence your will, but see what little power he has once you have given Me control of your mind? Once the decision was made it was easy. "My yoke is easy and my burden is light" (Matt. 11:30).

This is the key to victory over every temptation that will ever beset you. The mind is Satan's playground, but once you give Me control of your mind the rest is easy. It will be easier each time, now that you see how simple it really is: 1. The desire to be obedient. 2. The decision to turn it over and leave it with Me. 3. Then comes the release . . . it's as simple as that!

Speak Lord

As the rushing waterfall cascades down and toward the sea, so is time rushing toward the end when time will turn into endless eternity. How you spend that eternity largely depends on what you do with your time here and now.

You have obtained your salvation, your name is written in the Book of Life. But there is more . . . there are greater victories to be won, and I want you at the front lines where the action is. You have sat for far too long and watched the battle from afar. The bigger the commitment, the bigger the reward. Doors are being opened for you, many doors. The ones you go through are up to you. I can lead, but you must follow. Trust Me to do what is best for you. Let Me make you into the person you were meant to be before time began. Get rid of all the preconceived ideas you have of yourself . . . it is nothing less than escapism. I can make you into whatever I want you to be . . . if you are willing.

You say I use people according to their personalities, and that is true, but with your concept of what your personality is, I could never use you for anything! I can, and I do, change personalities when willingly submitted to Me.

Close the gap tighter now between who you are and who you should be. You are pleasing to Me now, but you are still far from who you will be.

I am bringing My Bride to perfection. Therefore, earnestly strive to examine your motives before you speak. Be very certain that what you are about to say can, in no way, be for the purpose of self-glorification.

You have told people of things you did "so you could pray about it" when the real reason you told them was so they would think highly of you! You have no need of man's praise, My child. A mind under the blood must be washed clean of all self glorification. Your motives must always be pure.

You have said you only want to pull the cords to open the curtain and reveal Jesus, and I know that is your heart . . . but be very careful, for in your best intentions the enemy can get in and distort your view, if you are not constantly on guard.

So, examine yourself before you speak and make very sure your motive is pure. If there is the slightest hint of self praise, it will not glorify Me, and it will be better left unsaid. You will have had all the glory you are going to get out of it! If your words glorify Me, your reward will be eternal. It is your choice.

Speak Lord

Come a step further up with Me now. Make a break with the past and do not be bound by meaningless traditions and customs. Do not get entangled with ritualistic form and lose sight of the substance. Ritual is beautiful if kept in its proper place. It must point to the end . . . it must not be the end itself. It is a thing to be used, you are not to let it use you.

You are called into a love relationship with the Lord of all Life, a personal commitment to a personal Savior. A surrender to the King of all ages.

The tools used to bring this relationship into focus are as many as there are different types of people. Be yourself . . . worship Me the way you, as an individual, feel most comfortable and at home. If your spirit feels like clapping, dancing, shouting, jumping . . . do it; otherwise . . . .be still. Just because all the others are jubilant doesn't mean this same moment for you cannot be one of quiet, meaningful communion with Me.

Listen to your heart and worship Me as you truly feel. While the crowd may be jumping, your spirit may want you to fall on your knees. Don't stifle that precious, tender feeling to follow the emotions of those around you! I love you all as individuals. I touch you all as individuals. I expect you to respond to Me as individuals. Follow the lead of your spirit.

I rejoice when My children are praising Me in one accord, with their emotions as one, but at the times when your heart is touched . . . or not touched (don't ever fake it), respond to the tug of your heart. If you don't, you will come away empty and robbed of what I had for you.

Remember, I want you to be one with Me and one with My body, but that does not mean I intend to rob you of the precious gift I gave you of your own separate, unique, individual walk with Me. You will become more united with Me and your brothers and sisters when you see your own true individuality growing and emerging as the butterfly from the cocoon, until you become all I intend you to be.

So, beloved, join in praise with My body, but also come apart with Me and listen as I speak to your heart. I have so many things to say to you!

Come before Me with singing and praise, for I have done a mighty work in you. I have folded the old filthy rags of your own righteousness and thrown them into the fire. "All our righteousness is like filthy rags" (Isa. 64:6). I have given you a new garment: My robe of righteousness. Be always aware of this and be thankful, for it is imparted righteousness. In no way are you deserving of this splendid attire . . . but it is yours, for you are Mine and, as a father clothes his children, so have I clothed you. Wear your new garment carefully, for it must not be soiled. Avoid the dirty things around you like the plague, for they must not come near My holiness.

Fear not the acts of others . . . only you can soil your garment, and I will not have My robe defiled. If anyone willingly dirties this robe, it will be taken from him. You are sanctified, you have been made pure and holy. Walk in this sanctification with love and with humility . . . never fearing what man says or thinks.

Walk in holiness, for I have called you to be holy. I have sanctified you by the washing of My blood. Remember, you are set apart. Never compromise in any way, no matter how trivial it may seem. There are no small sins.

Be honest with yourself. Be on the alert for ways to serve Me and of the deceptive ways of the enemy. My Spirit speaks to warn, encourage, and lead. You have in you a warning device put there by My Spirit. Heed these signals; if you are listening, they are loud and clear.

These things I tell you so that you may prepare for My coming. "Be anxious over nothing" (Phil. 4:6). Do not fear for those who will not be ready when I come . . . they have all been warned, and no one will be left who would be willing to be Mine.

You will rejoice in that day, and your heart will be full, for your heart's desires will be manifested. You will only regret one thing: The concern, the fear, the dread you had for so long that those for whom your heart yearned would be left to face times of terror and pain and, worse, to give in to it and be forever lost in all the horrors of hell. No, beloved, on that day you will be at peace, on that day you will know I am faithful and true . . . and I keep My word.

Every word in the Bible is true . . . every promise will be fulfilled. I have not forgotten any of My promises; they are as true today as they ever were. Trust Me and wait . . . I will not be late.

Speak Lord

Come into My presence this morning with a song in your heart, with words of praise on your lips, and with joy radiating from every cell of your body, for you truly do have every reason to be joyful.

Have I not promised you a life of peace . . . and an ever growing awareness of Me? Trust Me. You see it happening, you are aware that I am doing a mighty work in you.

Have no fear. No, you cannot handle it . . . but I can . . . and I will. Trust Me more and more. I have never broken a promise to you, and I never will.

Walk on that ever ascending road. Forsake the path of mountain-valley/mountain-valley travel. Satan uses the fake assumption that after each mountaintop experience there has to be a valley to defeat those who travel this way.

The valleys are there, but in your spirit you are not confined to the laws of nature, you need not follow the pathway down, but rather My angels can, and will, bear you safely across to the next mountaintop without any need for you to descend into the valley. You employ them by trusting Me, believing the word . . . and acting on it.

Come as a child to your Father. Climb upon My lap, rest your head on My chest, listen to My heartbeat, feel My strong arms around you . . . rest in Me. I will give you all the rest you need, for I am the Source of that rest.

"Be not weary in well doing" (2 Thess. 3:13). If you are in My will, you will never be overextended, for I provide for your every need. I am your strength, and I have promised to renew (and keep on renewing) your youth as an eagle (Ps. 103:5). As the eagle soars through the air with might in his wings, so I pour My vitality into you. "Those who wait upon the Lord shall renew their strength, they shall mount up with wings like eagles, they shall run and not be weary, they shall walk and not faint" (Isaiah 40:31).

Whenever you need anything, don't seek that thing itself, seek the Source, and I will be your supply. Do you need rest? Seek the Source of Rest. Do you need money? Seek the Source of Wealth. Do you need peace? Seek the Prince of Peace. Do you need love? Seek the King of Love. Joy? Health? . . . whatever your soul hungers for . . . seek it not in itself, for it will elude you. Seek Me . . . and all these things will be added unto you.

Speak Lord

"Arise, shine, for thy Light is come, and the glory of the Lord has risen upon thee" (Isaiah 60:1).

Come, come into the Holy of Holies, worship at the throne of grace. Abide in the presence of the most high God . . . your Daddy.

Arise, lay aside the grace clothes, stand strong as the new creation you are in Me. Come, leave the mundane behind, leave the world behind and the things that would so easily ensnare you. Abide in the presence of a holy God. Rise above the natural and abide in the supernatural, abide in Me.

Come as a little child to your Father. Come and be loved, protected, encouraged, fortified, and fed. Come and receive strength and cool water to quench your thirst. Come and receive forgiveness, comfort, peace. I have all this for you . . . and much, much more.

You are so very special to Me. I desire to hold back nothing from you . . . hold back nothing from Me.

So now . . . obey, My precious one. Come into the Holy of Holies and take up residence there . . . for you are not of this world, even as I am not of this world. Be confident of this one thing: Your life is hid with Me . . . and your life is safe in Me.

"Come, you blessed of My Father, inherit the kingdom prepared for you from the foundation of the world" (Matt. 25:34). You are a part of that kingdom, and I am your ever-present King. I execute justice and mercy for you, not only in this world, but in the world to come.

As a full fledged citizen of My kingdom, you have total protection given you by the King and His court (My angels). Harbor no fearful thoughts, for I, your God, am King and Ruler of all. I have all power in heaven and on earth . . . and you are My child . . . and I love you.

Come and walk in the shadow of My cross. Only there will you find what your soul longs for, there and only there will you be satisfied. I have laid down My life for you, and, because of that, you will have life eternal. I claim you for My own. Trust Me, believe in Me, and great will be your reward. I give you what the world cannot give, and I love you with a love that cannot be compared to anything that can be found in the world.

"Greater love has no one than this, than to lay down one's life for his friends" (John 15:13). You are My friend, My beloved child. Receive My love and you receive My life.

Speak Lord

Come and walk closely with Me. Keep your hand in Mine, I will make the rough paths straight. I will pick you up when you fall. I will always be as close as you want Me to be.

The battle has only begun, but you have all you need to win. Put on the whole armor of God, and I will keep you in all things. I will not cause My children to suffer unnecessarily.

Walk humbly and be filled with righteousness. Take no thought for tomorrow, I have upheld you so far; I will never let you go.

My ways are not your ways, My timing not your timing. Only put your whole trust in me, and I will bring it all to pass.

There will be much you will not be able to understand now . . . someday you will. On that day you will say: "Of course, why didn't I see that!" You say that now about things you were blind to a year ago.

There are spiritual truths that the mind of man cannot grasp . . . the spirit only can understand. If anyone tries to come to Me by way of his mind, he will lose Me. The things of God can only be found through the understanding of the spirit.

Only call upon Me and I will hear you and show you great and mighty things you have never dreamed of.

I am leading you now into realms you never even knew existed! This is not because of what you have done, nor of who you are, but because of Who I am and what I have done. I try My chosen ones in the areas where they need strengthening, and when the lesson has been learned, it is time to move on. You are about to move on now.

Today you go higher. As you go further from any object it becomes smaller; so, as you go further from the world, it will become more and more insignificant, and as you grow closer to Me, the things of the Spirit loom ever larger. The only area where this is not true is in the area of sin. The further away you get from it, and the closer to Me you are, the more conscious you become of the horrors of sin.

You have the victory in your life within your grasp now. No longer search for pennies when "the gold is Mine and the silver is Mine, saith the Lord" (Haggai 2:8)... and you are a joint heir with Jesus to it all!

Speak Lord

Come into My arms in loving trust, like a little child climb up onto My lap; nestle there and listen to My heartbeat.

Listen as I tell you of My love for you in the roar of the waves . . . in the gentle breeze ruffling the petals of a tiny flower . . . in the smell of fresh air and newly cut grass . . . the sweet aroma of orange blossoms . . . of hay. Listen to the beauty of a human voice sweetly singing, the voice of a loved one. Listen to soft sweet music, touch the cheek of a baby . . . a leaf . . . a tiny kitten . . . the bark of an old tree.

See the beauty in all My creation: a country scene . . . one flower . . . a bouquet . . . a human face . . . an animal . . . the sky . . . one cloud.

Sense My presence in quiet . . . in noise . . . in people . . . in the city . . . in the country . . . in the water . . . in the feel and smell of fresh air. Taste My love for you in the goodness of flavor of foods I have made enjoyable for no other reason but because I love you and delight in your pleasure.

Appreciate beauty in everything, in the arrangements of the feathers on a bird . . . of an orchestra. All things fitting together to form a whole . . . a creation of beauty. Stop, look, and listen.

Really see, really taste, really appreciate all the many things that are demonstrations of My love, given to you here and now. Do this and your sense of values . . . and all your senses . . . will be quickened to receive more, both here and hereafter.

If you were the only person I had ever created, I still would have made waterfalls, birds . . . all nature . . . everything . . . just for you. Don't get too busy to enjoy all I have created out of My overflowing love for you.

Come and wash in the fountain of life. Come and be refreshed now. I love you so much more than you can imagine! Be pleased with what you have but also look ahead to greater blessings.

Your financial needs are being met. You have trusted every area of your life to Me, so be sure of Me and know that because I give in one area does not mean I will not give in another. I can only give in the areas you have turned over to Me. So, search your heart and know I will supply your every need, and your every want, if your wants are pure and right in My sight.

Speak Lord

Come into the garden now while the dew of the Spirit rests gently upon the flower of faith. Pick the bouquet I have for you. Take the rose in all its beauty, with the bud of promise ready to bloom into your glorious tomorrow, with its thorns carefully placed by the One Who loves you most. You can avoid being hurt by these thorns if you carefully watch where you place your hands. Smell the fragrance . . . it too is a promise that every desire will be met and find its culmination in Me. "I see the Lord, He is high and lifted up" (Isa. 6:1).

Walk through My garden now while the dew of the Spirit rests gently upon the earth. Pick and eat of the fruit I offer you. The fruits of the Spirit lie within easy grasp. Taste and see how healing it is to feast on them. Let your spirit be attuned to My Spirit, to the sounds around you . . . the cry of the birds, the rustle of the wind in the trees. Hear Me speak to you through your physical ears, as well as through your spirit.

Walk through the garden and touch Me . . . and then go inside to the crowd and touch them . . . and they will touch you, and when they do, say to them: "Come into the garden . . . there is Someone there I want you to meet."

Can a child forget the mother who bore him? Can the fruit of her womb dismiss the life who brought him into the world? If he does forget, it is only because of the pain there is in remembering.

Do not despair; continue in the role in which I have placed you. I, the Producer and Director of the drama that is your life, will not loosen My grip on the reins. I will not leave you comfortless. "I will never leave you nor forsake you" (Heb. 13:5). I will never put more on you than you can bear. "Press on to the high calling of God in Christ Jesus" (Phil. 3:14). Keep your eye on the prize.

I am about to bring you help in your efforts. help that will come from a source as yet unknown to you. Trust Me and don't despair. You are not wasting your life . . . you are imparting your life. Be constant, be consistent. Turn to Me in those moments just before you speak. I will give you My words for the situation.

The enemy would have you believe you are failing, but I tell you, you can say, along with Paul: "There is laid up for me the crown of righteousness, which the Lord, the righteous Judge, will give me on that day" (2 Tim. 4:8).

So rejoice, My child, that day is at the door!

Speak Lord

The God of all ages has visited you.
The Creator God, the Father God . . . the Suffering Servant.
The Great I AM.
I have come that you may have life and have it abundantly. Blessed are you, for you have sought after me, and I have promised I will be found by those who seek Me. So seek Me even more diligently, for the level you achieve in seeking Me, is that level you will find Me. No one searches for Me with a pure heart and true intent who does not find Me.

Seek Me while I can still be found.

Tell the lost there will come a time when they will seek after Me and they will not be able to find Me, for they can only come when the Spirit draws them . . . not when they decide to come.

You have come, you have tasted the sweetness of the fruit of the tree of life. But you have only tasted, beloved. I say unto you, come; eat freely of the fruit I offer you; let nothing stand in the way. I have so much for you now that you are ready to eat and drink of My life. Come then, My child, and partake of the joy, the inexpressible, overflowing, abundant, unending, and exuberant joy of the Lord!

Prepare ye the way, for I am coming soon. Much sooner than you realize. I am coming to receive My Bride to Myself. I am coming in the clouds of glory, and the dead in Christ shall rise first, and then you, beloved, you shall be caught up in the air . . . and so shall you ever be with Me.

The excitement is building up even now in you, as it is in all My people who have heard and understand this message. Take no thought for tomorrow; there will not be too many more tomorrows in this stage of your development. Your tomorrows will be spent with Me, and all thought for that tomorrow will be Mine, for the Bridegroom takes good care of His Bride, and she will have a full and abundant eternity.

The Bridegroom is even now at the gate! On that day what will you care for money? Where will your pain be? Where did your tears go? For in that day all need, pain, and death will be swallowed up in victory! So be patient; love those around you with My love, and then wait for Me, watch for Me, and, in the fullness of time, I will come for you. There is only yet a little while and you will see Me. This is My promise to you. You long to see Me, and see Me you will. I am waiting, even now to come for you.

Precious and few are the days that are left. The countdown has begun, and you are part of My endtime plan for the salvation of as many as will come to Me. Be alert, be prepared to be used at a moment's notice. This is why I tell you to keep close, for you will be called upon when you least expect it. You will not fail Me if you keep close and keep the channel clear and clean. There is still much to be done and very little time to do it.

Your willingness is received by Me, and it will not go unused. Look up, for your salvation is at hand, yes, even at the door.

Drop all fear as you would a filthy garment. There is no need to fear, there is no time to be hampered by it. Replace the stagnant garment of fear with the pure, fresh smelling robe of righteousness. This robe, when worn with the mantle of praise and the armor of God, ensures that you are completely protected.

So take up your battle station, My little warrior; march under the banner of the cross and know for a fact that you cannot lose. Step boldly into the battle, the war has already been won. It is just for you now to receive the victor's reward from the Victor King Himself!

Do not be impatient. I am manifesting myself through you, but it is usually not in the way you think. You may be speaking to someone about Me and you may feel discouraged because you don't think the seed has taken root. What you don't see, however, is someone sitting nearby who heard what you said and your words fell like dynamite on their ears . . . and their life was changed!

I use that as an example. Don't put Me in a box. Be flexible . . . do what you are led to do and don't bear the responsibility for the outcome. You are not asked to save anyone; you are only asked to introduce them to the Savior. You are not asked to bear the brunt of the load . . . it is Mine, not yours. So be happy, be free, be open, you are of more use than you know.

Time spent in My service may not be consciously spent actively doing My work. A look, a touch, done in My love, speaks silently of Me and stirs the heart of the hungry, whether they are aware of it or not. They feel a lack in themselves, and they will look at your life to see where you are getting it from. Sometimes a word unspoken but seen in the eyes, the deeds and the touch of those who are in touch with Me, speak louder than a mighty sermon.

Gently reflect My love.

Speak Lord

"Come unto Me all ye that labor and are heavy laden, and I will give you rest" (Matt. 11: 28). This promise is for now and for any time you ever need to appropriate it.

All My promises are meant for you as much as they were meant for the people to whom the messages were given. That is what is meant by "the word is alive" . . . not only is it as meaningful today as it ever was (for My message is timeless), but it also means that each promise is alive for each person individually, just as if I were speaking them to you today. My words are eternal, alive, not "mere words on paper written hundreds of years ago; that in some cases can apply to us today." No! My word is ever fresh, ever new, and alive. It has power—power to heal, power to save, power to destroy, and power to convict.

Look upon My word in a new light. Have it speak to you as if it was written especially for you . . . it was. Allow Me to minister life to your spirit through My word. Don't look at the Bible as a group of stories. You will only begin to understand its power once you begin to see it for what it really is. You will understand its power only as you use it more and more. It will minister life to you . . . for it is alive.

Come to Me empty-handed. Let your mind be concentrated only on Me. Lift your empty cup, and I will fill it so full you will feel like saying: "Stop, enough" . . . but you won't, because the drink will be so sweet you will want more and more. My gifts can satisfy completely; but even as they satisfy, you will want still more.

This journey does not stop at the end of this phase of your existence. You will continue growing and being conformed more and more into the image of My Son. That cannot happen overnight, but the more earnestly you seek My perfection the quicker you will arrive. It is like running a race: you are in a hurry to get to the goal, yet when you have setbacks or when you fall, you must get back on track as quickly as possible and make up for lost time.

Your life now is but a walk toward the rest. Perfection is the goal, but that is not attained during the walk, only at the destination. So keep on walking, My beloved. Even though the road may sometimes seem too tiring, too monotonous, keep the goal in mind, it won't be long. You know motivation is the key to any successful endeavor, and to arrive a winner in the Eternal City is the highest motivation anyone can have! You have your motivation . . . now keep on running and you will win the prize.

Speak Lord

I want you to be part of My "road crew," paving the way before Me, preparing the ground for My return. Don't be anxious about this. I will equip you. The groundwork is laid, the foundation is down; you are to be one who will pave the way. Be ready for action. You are anxious to see everyone saved, but you can't do it that way. I will send those to whom you are to minister . . . wait for my signal.

Remember the parable of the sower. The seed sown on unfertile ground will only wither away. Through My Spirit in you, I will show you (if only you will listen) who is the right person, when is the right time, and what is the right way. If you don't feel My Spirit leading, then only pray for that person until their time is ripe. I know how you feel, but don't be over anxious . . . nothing is accomplished that way.

I want you to be one of My "fishermen," but unless the bait, the weather, and the time is right, you won't catch any fish. I don't want you to be a discouraged fisherman, so wait for the conditions to be right, and I promise you, your net will be full to overflowing!

Practice letting the mind of Christ dwell richly in you. "What would Jesus think about this? How would He respond? What would His answer be? How can I be more like Him?" Only by knowing Me, My character, My will, can you become more like Me. Being conformed to My image is not an instant action or transaction like salvation; but rather it is a slow process of growing, whereby the seeker grows closer and closer to the beloved . . . coming ever nearer, more and more being conformed into His likeness.

When an actor accepts a role portraying another human being, if he is to be successful, he must learn all he can about this person: his habits, his likes and dislikes, his deep feelings . . . what makes him happy, what makes him sad . . . where he likes to go, what he likes to do . . . how he looks, how he feels, how he speaks, how he spends his time . . . everything he can about that person. To the extent that he masters all these things, only then can he truly reflect the image he desires to portray.

Being "conformed into My image" (Romans 8:29) goes far deeper than that and takes a lifetime of commitment. But oh, beloved, the rewards are far, far greater than your mind can even begin to grasp! Begin today!

Speak Lord

Being a Christian means being a "little Christ." Do you know what that means? You not only portray Me as someone from the outside, but you beam forth out of you what is already in you. Because, as My own, I dwell in you, and it only remains for you to allow that which dwells deeply within you to shine forth as the sun. Allow no blockage to mar the manifestation of Who I am in you.

Pride, sin, selfishness, unworthiness, all block your revelation of Me; so put these things where they belong, in the rubble under the cross, and go on with Me.

I became sin so that you could become the righteousness of God. Have I died for you in vain in that area? So then, where is your sin? If you have truly died with Me and risen to new life, pride and selfishness will have been buried with the old life, and where you truly were unworthy, I have made you worthy with My worthiness. So, beloved, lay aside that which is only another distorted side of pride, and step into trust in My worthiness in you.

For I have called My children for this end: to be the revelation of Jesus Christ to the world.

Come and be alone with Me, for now is a time of refreshing. Bring your cares, your tiredness, your depression, your longings . . . bring them to Me now.

"Behold, I stand at the door and knock" (Rev. 3:20) with My arms open wide and ready to take from you all that oppresses you . . . ready to take and bear for you each and every occasion where you have been so hurt, so wounded by those you love the most. Eagerly I would take all this from you.

I know how it feels to hurt; I understand rejection. I was rejected when I needed love and help the most: "They all forsook Him and fled" (Mark 14: 50). No one has ever been more misunderstood than I was, nor more human in My need to be understood.

So, now My child, I understand . . . and I am to you, and for you, all you need in this area of your life. I take from you all that would bruise, sting, poison, or grieve your spirit in any way, but you must give it to Me immediately before it has a chance to take root. Turn to Me as soon as it happens; don't give it time to fester within you. As you receive a hurt, literally throw it at Me . . . I haven't missed a catch yet and I never will!

Speak Lord

When someone you love is thoughtless, returning hurt instead of praise, coldness and rejection instead of love, refuse to accept it! Treat it like a hot potato and throw it to Me! Once the fire of My love consumes it, you are free from the effects that could have been so devastating.

Return unequivocal love instead of receiving hurt. Satan wants to use those dearest to you to destroy your spirit. But, oh My precious one, you are far removed from his power now! So stand in the victory of the cross of Calvary and know the joys and the power that is rightfully yours as a joint heir with Jesus to the kingdom of glory.

You still haven't learned to trust Me fully yet. You limit Me, you stay My hand. Give Me free rein; let My power loose; release it completely, so I can work unhampered in your life. The degree you doubt is the degree to which you limit Me. Burst from your prison of doubt and be free to accept your full inheritance and live as you were meant to live: a victorious, healthy, joyful, peaceful life.

Replace sin, sorrow, and sickness with surrender, salvation and sanctification. First surrender to Me, then will come full salvation and sanctification. Allow Me to make you all I created you to be.

Are you weary? Then pour yourself out. Some weariness comes from giving too much, some from not giving enough.

Weariness comes from many sources: hurts, disappointments, frustrations, unfulfilled desires, not enough sleep, medications, illness, tedious work, or too much physical activity too fast. You know how to deal with each and every one of these things, so walk in that knowledge now.

Now pour yourself out to and for others, and, as you are emptied, I will fill you in deeper, richer ways than ever before.

Your roots go deep in rich, fertile soil, and the rains serve only to make your roots absorb the nourishment. So, when the rains fall, be thankful, for it is making you grow faster, and I need to bring you to full growth as quickly as possible.

You have come to a point in your life that is not a crossroad, but rather it is the end of the road that you know and are accustomed to travel. The road has stopped abruptly in front of you. You say: "I cannot go on, I cannot go back, I cannot go left nor right. I am alone." Now, beloved, look up! The pathway is even now being cleared for the new road. So, stand still, look up, and wait.

Speak Lord

Be aware of My life in you in a fuller way; allow that life to have full and free expression. Come to my banqueting table and feast with Me. You never need to hunger nor thirst . . . physically, mentally, emotionally, nor spiritually.

I am your Source, your strong High Tower. I feel with you. I am not an inanimate object inside of you, I live within you. I am active, vibrantly alive in you, and, with My coming, you were also made far more alive; take advantage of this . . . be aware of this vibrant, pulsating life in you and live life to its fullest.

I am never tired . . . tap into My strength. I am never bored, overworked, nor restless. I want to impart all of Who I am to you. Be righteous, for I am righteous. Be holy, for I am holy. Be love, for I am love.

You need to begin to develop your spiritual side more. Die to self and all its limitations. Look to Me for everything. Ask Me your questions, turn everything over to Me. I love you, and I want to be in control of your life so that you will know what perfect joy, perfect peace, and complete fulfillment is. Wherever you are, whatever you are doing, if you have put all in My hands, you will see what I mean.

The restlessness in your soul is due to alienation from Me. The more you are conformed to My image the less there is to cloud your true self.

The frustrations, the questions that puzzle you, all the areas that cloud who you really are, will melt away as the true child of God emerges and stands in the glory of My presence. So, be who you are: that precious, saved, cherished, protected Bride for whom the Bridegroom laid down His life and for whom He comes again in great power and glory to call to His side.

You know I am your hiding place, your protection. "I am the Way, the Truth, and the Life" (John 14:6). Walk only in the light I provide, and I will always be there to fill your every need. The more of Me you appropriate, the deeper will be your joy. Do not think I am come to rob you of the joys this life has to offer. I have far more and deeper joys awaiting you. Wait and watch, feel and see, and experience the joys I send with My blessings upon them. Then, beloved, you will look back, and how you will rejoice at the choice you made to follow Me!

Why do you walk under the shadow of uncertainty and doubt when you are already walking under the shadow of My umbrella of protection?

Speak Lord

Think about this concept of salvation: you have fallen into a pit of snakes with lions surrounding it, and fire closing in on you. Suddenly the rains come, and the fire goes out, the thunder scares away the lions, but you still can't get out. Your every hope is gone . . . and the snakes are getting closer! Suddenly to hear a voice: "Stretch out your hand and I will pull you out." Would you say no?

Yet many say "no" to a far greater salvation! Far more than that has been done for you, far more than you can understand. Would anyone reject this rescue? Would anyone say: "No, I want to stay here and take my chances?" Would anyone pull his hand away from the outstretched arms of the Rescuer? No? Yet many do just that. Yes or no . . . it must be one or the other. All that is needed is: "Yes, I will follow You. I will stretch out my hand and take Yours. I will allow You to save me."

My Spirit will not always strive with your spirit. Stretch out your hand now while there is yet time . . . while Mine is still reaching out for you. "How shall we escape if we neglect such great salvation?" (Heb. 2:3).

Practice My presence, listen for My guidance, watch over My little ones. Help the helpless, be the strength of the weak, the joy of the sorrowful, and the hope of the hopeless.

Build the faith of those to whom I send you. Love the unlovable, guide the lost back to the fold. Look for a need and fill it, and you will be truly serving Me. Concentrate on losing yourself and finding more and more of Me.

Precious are you, and blessed, for you seek after My will to obey it. Truly I do see your heart, I know your motives, I understand far more than you do the driving forces behind all your actions. Many of these driving forces were put there by Me for your pleasure. Satan abuses, but the child of God uses. Use to My glory that which you have been given. You alone know what I mean, you alone know how to do this.

To him that overcomes I will give the right to reign on high with Me. You are fast becoming the overcomers I have called you to be.

Your will is the key. Allow Me to turn that key in the door and lock it against the temptations of the deceiver. Remember always to say when he knocks at the door: "Jesus, please answer the door for me." That is the way the victory is won.

"Enter into His gates with thanksgiving, and into His courts with praise" (Ps. 100:4). Be joyful and express My joy. Come and be the person I have called you to be, for you are My life extended on earth. You are My feet and My hands, you are My voice.

How beautiful and precious are My children to Me! How it grieves My Spirit when you live beneath your inheritance!

Follow and believe those who preach the victorious Christian life. The victory truly was won for you at Calvary, and part of that victory was meant for the here and now of your life. Let it not have been in vain!

If you allow defeat to defeat you, then you allow the cross to have been a wasted experience for you in that area of your life. Do not the sufferings of My Son for you deserve more than that? Do not ignore the cross! For every area where you allow defeat in your life, that is an area where you are ignoring the agony and the victory of the cross.

Receive now, beloved, every benefit given you by the experience of the cross, and let not My Son's death be in vain for you in any way. Live in the victory won for you at Calvary.

Hold fast to what you believe, in spite of all opposition. In the midst of the storm, there is a hiding place of great safety and calm. You have no need to fear. You are under the protection of My angels who are sent to minister unto you. They will refresh you, surround you, and uphold you.

There is nothing to fear . . . no loss, no terror in the night. Raise your faith level to where you walk consistently in all the promises afforded you in Psalm 91. You must be very sure of this. I do not draw and then repel. I have drawn you . . . you have responded. This is all that I need.

Stop straining at the bit! You are like an unbridled horse . . . anxious to go, but not sure where! Wait until you feel the tug of My reins . . . wait until you feel Me show you which way I want you to go.

You are saddled, blinders on; your Master is in command. Wait for My lead. I know where I want you to go, and only I know when and how you are to go. I will not allow you to go astray. Get used to following My lead. Instead of being a runaway, you will be a champion! Wait for the lead, and then follow Me wherever I lead you. You will know when I am in command, and you will learn to follow without hesitation or doubt.

Thoroughbreds act the part!

Don't ever feel lost in the crowd, in the multitudes before My throne. You are as special to Me as if you were the only one there! Be confident of that special relationship we have and know I love you no more when you are "being good" and shining your light for the world to see than I do when you are "not feeling good" and hiding in a corner. You are no less important to Me then . . . no less special.

My love envelopes you . . . surrounds you . . . insulates you. My arms enfold, uphold, and comfort you. My power dwells in you no less powerfully in affliction. You are Mine, unequivocally, unquestionably, unfailingly. Yes, you fail, but that never changes the fact that you are Mine.

I have you eternally in the palm of My hand. I will nourish, restrict, empower, subdue, bring forward, hold back, to the degree necessary in all things. I am your refuge and your strength. Your steps will never falter as long as your hand is in Mine. There is still a long road ahead, but I will make the path clear and straight, and I will give you all you need to complete the journey.

You are learning about trust . . . now learn about abandonment. You are about to receive one of the greatest blessings I have ever given you . . . reach out and take it.

You have done all you need to do, you have surrendered to Me. Now allow Me to take over. I have never failed you . . . I never will.

I am not a garment to be tried on for size and if I fit and feel comfortable you decide to leave Me on. No, I am either all or nothing! Decide to make Me all, and all My promises become yours, and I fill you to overflowing. Can I be Lord over just certain selected areas of your life? Beloved, I am Lord of all . . . or I am not your Lord at all.

This is not a principle to be tried to see if it works. With that attitude, it never would! I meant it when I said that I am a jealous God, and I know what works for you. Make Me all in all, and you will not be able to contain the blessings I will pour upon you!

This is a way of life that is undertaken . . . a decision made to live for Me. Remember Job's words: "Though He slay me, still will I trust Him" (Job 13:15). That is the attitude of heart it takes to make it all come together for you. Then, and only then, will you walk in the fullness of all I have in store for you.

My gifts are for now, not for some time in the future. If I have to hold back a blessing from you it is not because I am slow to act, it is because there is something in your life that is preventing the manifestation of the blessing.

You have just removed another block! You can receive more now. You will receive more now, for I am swift to act once the way is clear. You now see that "in God's timing" does not mean anything more than "when you are able to receive it." If there is a block, and you are willing to have it removed, I can work in the twinkling of an eye! I can undo in that time all the damage that took years to grow, like a cancer, inside of you.

I destroy now all the hindrances to abundance in the fullest sense of the word, for you have given Me this freedom. You need no longer be patient, for the time of fulfillment has come! All you need to do now is receive. Be like a dry sponge and just soak up all I have for you now . . . today.

Behold, today salvation has come to your house! Now is the appointed time . . . now is the day of salvation . . . salvation from sin, sickness, poverty, unhappiness. Today is the day of glory!

My child, you put boulders in your own pathway, and when you trip over them you wonder why!

You have been taught the spiritual principle: "Act as if it already were, and it shall be" . . . now practice it! Act as if you love Me more today than you did yesterday. Act as if you know Me more today than you did yesterday. Act as if you serve Me better now than then. Act as though you love all My children. Act as if it is . . . and it will be. You truly do seek first the Kingdom of God, but now you need to stop denying the power that is within you.

You are making the enemy play havoc with your thoughts and your emotions—why do you allow this? You are totally outside of his domination, yet you give heed to his lies. Be done with this once and for all.

I need My children to grow up. I need maturity in My body. I cannot allow you to stay where you are any longer. I call you to grow into full Christian maturity now, for I desire to use you more fully, but you tie My hands.

How can you minister meat while you still feed on baby food yourself?

Speak Lord

My people, your present life is but the preface to the book of your life . . . a story that will never end . . . a love story of unparalleled beauty, the story of My Bride-to-be, now living on Planet Earth. You are on the page now where she is awaiting her own true love, and although she is not aware of it, He is on the verge of coming for her! He is about to take her to live forever with Him, in a life of glory far beyond her capacity to envision!

Read each page with joy and expectancy, knowing that whatever happens on the next page is there because the Author wanted it to be there, and He alone knows best how this story should be written. Read this story with peace in your heart because you know the Author, and you know His love for you, and you know how the story will end.

This is a book written in love, about the Author of Love Himself, and His love for His Bride . . . it is a love story, it is your story. So read with great interest and excitement, wondering joyfully what the Lover of your soul has in store next for His Church: His beloved Bride.

You have inherited a kingdom! Depending on where you are on the road, this kingdom can be either near or far. The name of this kingdom is: Victorious Living. Living in Victorious Kingdom has nothing to do with salvation . . . whether you ever attain this kingdom on earth or not, the heavenly kingdom awaits all of My redeemed.

This Victorious Kingdom is where you can be while still in this phase of your existence. It is not too far away from where you are now.

There is a highway for you to travel; it is called the Highway of Faith. As you travel this road you will see there are many roads crossing it, many of which will seem to be the way to go. The main intersection is where faith meets doubt; and many, thinking this is the way they should go, will be sidetracked into the wrong path. They will turn at doubt, thus turning away from faith. It is as though faith runs north and south, and doubt runs east and west. Many will try to reach the Kingdom of Victorious Living by the road called Doubt, but you can never reach north by heading east or west.

There will be many intellectuals on this road, for they believe they must prove something before it is to be believed. My word is the final authority.

Believe Me when I say "Blessed are those who have not seen . . . and yet have believed" (John 20:29).

Speak Lord

There are many signposts on the road leading to Victorious Living, many are erected by the enemy to deceive and lead you onto the wrong path. But you have the roadmap I have given you: My word. You have the witness of My Spirit in your spirit, and you have the wisdom of those who have traveled this pathway before you.

Receive into your spirit only images implanted by My word of faith and those around you who speak it.

Keep going in the direction you know is the right way to go, according to the directions you have received from the King of this kingdom. You have been sent a special invitation to come and dwell with Him in His kingdom; you will find it in the roadmap He has provided for you.

The doors are open wide. Let nothing, let no one detract or deter you. You must take the journey yourself; but look ahead... look at the lives of those who dwell in that kingdom now and follow in their footsteps.

Make a positive decision now to walk the road called Perfect Faith. This is the shortcut... try it and see how fast it takes you to the kingdom!

There are other crossroads along the road to the Kingdom of Victorious Living that can lead you astray in a very subtle manner.

The road called Hope has side roads that lead into the road called Doubt. In many instances, Hope intersects with Faith.

Hope speaks of the future. When you hope for something, it is not yet within your grasp. Faith believes that it is . . . not that it will (or may) be. "Faith is the substance of things hoped for, the evidence of things not seen" (Hebrews 11:1). It is here, now, in the present. Tomorrow never comes!

You hold onto hope until you have confirmation from My word that you what you desire is My will for you. Once you receive that, it is already yours. All you need to do now is have the faith that in My perfect timing it *will* be manifested.

"Whatsoever things ye desire, when ye pray, believe that *you have them* (not that you will have them), and you shall have whatsoever ye desire" (Mark 11: 24). You need never "hope" you will receive what I have promised to give you in My word! Am I not faithful to My word? Will I not fulfill all I have promised?

Speak Lord

The faith I want you to have is not faith in the answered prayer but faith in the God Who answers prayer. Keep your eye on Me and not on what the outcome of your prayer will be.

Again, I say I respond to your faith in Me ... not to your faith in the answer to the prayer! Believe that you will receive because you have met the conditions: you regard not iniquity in your heart, but you know on Whom you have believed, and you are confident that He is able to do that which He has promised. I always finish what you start in prayer!

Do you fear the prayer will not be answered and you will be ashamed and made to look foolish ... or are you afraid that I will? Beloved, My reputation does not stand or fall on what you do! I am able to redeem all the mistakes My children make when they step out in faith in My name.

Your failures are turned into victories, for I see the intent of your heart. Expect answers to your prayers ... definite, specific prayers. If you will consciously live for Me, you will get your prayers answered. Your prayers go through the "hot line" that is established at salvation. That line is always open, unless you fail to pay the price to keep it installed. The price I charge is to live inside My perfect will for your life.

Can you not accept the fact that the Creator of all things can also re create? "Behold, I make all things new" (Rev. 21:5). I make you a new creature . . . a child of the Kingdom of Heaven, no more of this world. What I have made that has become defiled or ruined, I can remake and bring to wholeness of life such as never before known.

Now is the accepted time . . . not sometime in the future. I only have one time, and that time is now.

Growing God-centered over being self-centered can be as slow or as fast a process as you want it to be. I stand ready to help you in every way, but so much depends on your will. I have given you freedom . . . you have to develop your will and then surrender that will over to Me completely. Then, and only then, can I be free to use you and to give you everything I have in store for you. Concentrate on that area now: total surrender of your will.

I am waiting with so many blessings for you that you won't be able to hold them! Step out and prove Me now.

Speak Lord

All knowledge, wisdom, love, and joy; all health—physical, mental and spiritual; all power, and all peace spring from Me . . . and you are Mine. Why, then are you living so far beneath your rights? Why do you continue to paddle around in three feet of water when I have given you wings to fly above the ocean?

Take Me at My word: "Call those things which are not as though they are . . . and they shall be" (Rom. 4:17). Satan can rob you only to the extent that you let him.

Have done then with kindergarten play! You were getting so close . . . get back to where you were! Speak My word in faith . . . you are not responsible for the outcome, I am. Remember, My reputation does not stand nor fall with you. Just be you . . . and let Me be God.

I have not called you to heal . . . I have called you to speak My words of healing. I have not called you to save . . . I have called you to speak My words of salvation and point them to the Savior. Don't accept responsibility for the answers to your prayers . . . that is My part.

Don't be deceived, for "that which a man sows will he also reap" (Gal. 6: 7). This is a governing principle that applies in every area of life, not just in finances. Sow discontented thoughts and you reap discontent. Sow seeds of love and you will reap love; of health and you will be healthy; of busyness and you will be busy.

How are seeds sown? "As a man *thinketh* in his heart, so is he" (Proverbs 23:7). *"Out of the abundance of the heart the mouth speaks"* (Matt. 12:34). First the thought, then the spoken word. The act is the result of the thought. Guard jealously your thought life, for from it you create life or death as your thoughts are formed into words. "Life and death are in the power of the tongue" (Prov. 18:21).

I have placed an angel as sentinel over your thoughts, but he will not act against your own will. If you sanction a thought and choose to think it, he must stand helplessly by; but if you refuse it, reject it, and, by an act of your own will, eject it, then he will do battle with those forces that continually seek to do you harm. Then you will no longer be the "helpless victim" of that idea, thought, or desire.

You know the way to victory—now take it!

"Just be led of the Lord." This is what you hear from many sides and it may lead to confusion.

Be careful; you can be deceived and led astray by the enemy, for he comes as an angel of light, and many, believing his voice to be the voice of authority, follow what seems to be so right . . . and they are led to slaughter.

Those who heed not the voice of the Good Shepherd are enticed by the seducing lies of the false shepherd, who counterfeits and blinds the eyes of all he can. He comes as a thief to steal, kill, and destroy, and lead the sheep to slaughter through a way that may seem so right and so good. "There is a way that seems right to a man, but its end is the way of death" (Prov. 14:12).

Be watchful lest you fall into temptation. Temptation takes on many colors, and sometimes you do just what you should not do, thinking you are avoiding the wrong path. The adversary is constantly scheming to fool you. The way of sin is often times strewn with roses, and the path of righteousness can seem thorny or barren. You can easily be fooled if you try to discern his plans on your own. Seek My will, and I will not let you make the wrong choice.

Two voices call to you: one is a call to die to self and be raised to newness of life. The other is a call to do whatever feels good and whatever your desires dictate. This is the call to the slaughterhouse . . . seducing, deceiving, sweet. Deadly poison is nestled into the cup of temptation.

The cup I offer may at times taste bitter, but as you drink deeply, the sweeter to your taste this drink will become. Sip from the cup of temptation and you will despair because of the knowledge of what lies ahead for you once you have drained the bitter dregs of the cup of death. Drink not unto condemnation but unto eternal life with Me, for My grace will abound in your mortal flesh unto immortality, and your spirit will be nourished with eternal food.

So when the call comes to drink from this cup, allow the Spirit of God to bear witness within your spirit that this is the way to go: "Can I take You, Lord Jesus, joyfully and freely into this situation with me and know that You will be comfortable there?"

Speak Lord

Drink deeply of the cup of the Lord: the cup of mercy, salvation, healing, forgiveness, holiness, and union with God. Take of this cup and drink of Me, and it shall be unto you springs of living water unto eternal life.

I want you to understand that I understand. I came not to condemn but that, through Me, you should be saved. You are in Me . . . I am in you.

You are not standing before Me to receive My condemnation, but to receive My forgiveness, My understanding, and My love.

If, in the eyes of the world, a sin has been committed, look to Me. If, in your heart, a sin has been committed, look to Me.

Guilt can stir repentance or it can cause mental breakdown, depending on what you choose to do with it.

When you love someone, it hurts you to hurt them. You love Me, but not enough, for you cannot see how sin hurts Me. You hate sin, but not enough, for you cannot see how sin hurts Me.

Today I give you that deeper love for Me and a greater awareness of what sin does to Me. Your life will change dramatically now, for you cannot know Me as I will allow you to know Me and remain the same.

Lay aside all thought of earthly treasure, for your treasure is laid up with Me in safekeeping, awaiting your homecoming.

The pleasures of this earth fade into nothingness as true riches become available. As your eye beholds the treasures of the Spirit, you will seek less and less of the temporal.

I will bless you here and now, yes . . . I have promised that to you, so you need take no more thought for tomorrow. I will provide in abundance for you. Now seek Me more . . . and earthly gain less, for therein lies your true wealth.

Will not an earthly father give to his children out of his abundance? How much more will I, the Owner of it all, give to My children out of the storehouse of My abundance!

Set your eyes, therefore, on the promised land, and, as you go, I will rain manna from heaven down upon you. That is not the end in itself; the prize, your true prize . . . the pearl of great price . . . the eternal reward is in My hands, and I hold it out to you. Reach for this, and when it is yours you will understand why I told you to settle for nothing less.

"Forgetting those things which are behind, let us reach forward to those things which are ahead" (Phil. 3:13). That is not always easy to do. Natural man is the sum total of his past. The hurts of the past bring the fears of the present. Natural man has nothing to rely on except his past experiences to guide him.

But you, beloved, you . . . come away now from all that hurts and all you dread because of the hurts of the past. "Behold I make all things new" (Rev. 21:5).

The old man, once crucified with Me, is no more . . . you are now a new creature in Me, and your past is not even your past anymore . . . it is the past of one who has died, one whose life is now hid in Me. You can be very impersonal about it; it no longer affects you . . . it no longer concerns you. That was a different person . . . you have risen to newness of life!

Live now in your new life: a newborn child of God . . . your sins washed away by My blood. "The life is in the blood" (Lev. 17:11). My blood has given you life. Transfused into glory, you have become alive into eternity!

Now it's time to move on! Stand up, ready to go when I call. You must be ready at a moment's notice, for you and I have much to accomplish together, and the time is ripe.

$\mathcal{B}$lessed are they which do hunger and thirst after righteousness, for they shall be filled" (Matt. 5:6). Nothing pleases Me more than to fill My hungry children with good things!

Oh, My child, if only you knew what glories lie ahead for you, if only you were able to grasp it! I would, with great joy, pour these revelations into your heart, yet I restrain My hand, for the smallest insight makes you discontent with where you are now. One small revelation of Me and you want to throw everything up in the air and run after some nebulous form of "serving Me." What would you do if I opened your spiritual eyes and ears to a full revelation of Me!

Mature, My precious child. Serve Me with your eyes and heart on Me and your feet planted firmly among My precious children who still walk in darkness. Walk among them in love, compassion, and service.

The glorious moments with Me that make you want to burst the cocoon and fly away are not meant to distract or deter you from living to the fullest the day I have set before you today.

Speak Lord

"For I know the plans I have for you, saith the Lord, plans for welfare and not for evil, to give you a future and a hope" (Jer. 29:11). I have called, and you have answered . . . you have called, and I have answered.

Pray and My Spirit will guide your understanding. Earnestly seek My truths, and you will be rewarded. Seek Me and you will be filled.

Have you ever come to Me with a question and not received the answer? Turn to Me with all your doubts and all your questions. Only in Me will you get the answers that satisfy your soul.

The time of waiting is almost over, the time of refreshment has come. The day of jubilee is fast approaching, and you will be ready.

Set sail, beloved. Stand strong at the helm with the wind in your face, not blowing you over, but invigorating you. The Captain is in charge. The anchor has been raised, the storm has passed. It is now time to set sail. All you need to do is stand . . . your Captain will do the rest. When He sends you, just obey. When He calls you, just stand by His side. Be ready and available. Listen to Him, not the wind. Look to Him, not the dark clouds, for they will all blow over. As you sail into unknown seas, all you need to do is trust and obey . . . and enjoy the trip!

I honor your commitment to Me as you become less and less a part of the world.

Your interests are beginning to lie above and beyond the temporal life and the things that entertain the world. The toys, with all their flaws, are being left behind. When My Spirit truly dwells in you, your spirit recoils and is repulsed by the things of the Kingdom of Darkness.

Be bold to stand firm for the truth as you know it. You are My ambassador, and I give you now more power, for you have withstood the trials and temptations that are a part of the level you are on now.

I will never lead you to choose the wrong way. I not only tell you the way to go . . . I go with you, all the way . . . your hand in Mine. I go ahead of you to clear the way; I walk beside you to be your strength and your companion. I walk behind you to protect you from unseen dangers. I am all you need.

So, beloved, come up higher . . . receive the power, the blessings, the insights that come with this new level, and, after you have conquered this, you will once again hear Me say: "Come, beloved, it's time to go higher."

Speak Lord

As the rose unfolds its petals at the caress of the sun, so My little ones are meant to open up their lives to the healing rays of My love and protection. There is a correlation between everything in nature and your spiritual life.

You go through the storms of life, yes, but you go under the shadow of My wings through the lashing wind and stinging rain; your spirit is left unharmed by the bits of hurling debris, and you will grow all the stronger for the experience. It is protection that can be likened to being in a glass bubble, but, unlike the glass bubble, My protection will not break, and it offers perfect freedom . . . freedom to become the person you were created to be.

I planned for you from before eternity began! How special does that make you? You were not just conceived nine months before your birth, you were conceived in the Spirit from the time of creation, and I have a beautiful plan for your life!

Stand tall and don't confine yourself to living only in the here and now; you have grown above having to do that. Live with Me now in eternity . . . above and beyond time and space.

Come out of your cocoon now, My little butterfly, and come and fly away with Me.

Call upon Me and I will hear you. Call My name and I will answer. I call you now to serve Me in the little things: The cup of cold water, the smile, the touch, the look. These may seem so unimportant, and you feel frustrated because you are not doing bigger things for Me. You don't yet know the impact you are having in many lives around you! In whatsoever state you find yourself, therein be content. That is My will for you.

It is not necessarily the things you do, but your willingness to do them that will be taken into account at the day of judgment. It is not your ability, but your availability for which I yearn.

Take one step at a time. Don't be in a hurry; be more thorough. Make sure you have grasped one truth before you pursue another. One truth firmly held is worth more than fifty loosely grasped and easily lost.

I see your heart. I understand, and I will not hold you accountable for things over which you have not been given any power; trust in the justice and mercy of your Heavenly Father.

Speak Lord

"Truly I say unto you, unless you become as little children you will never enter the Kingdom of Heaven" (Matt. 18:3). Why? Why do I want My people to be as little children?

Who are they, these little people I love so dearly? A child is totally dependent, totally trusting. They don't worry about what to wear or where their next meal is coming from. They have an inborn trust that everything will be all right. I can move freely when My people think like that!

A child responds to love and loves back, freely, with no reservation, a pure, sweet, and simple love. A child is naturally gentle (unless there are circumstances that have warped his personality and outlook). He will care for those who need him. Watch a little girl as she lovingly tends her doll. A child is pure, uncomplicated, forgiving. A child does not worry, does not care about being considered a person worthy of the head seat at the table. He would rather sit on the floor! A child is open and responsive, with a natural instinct in him that (unless crushed by his surroundings) will lead him to seek Me.

Become then as little children: joyful, innocent, trusting, knowing that I am always near, and you are always protected.

*B*ehold, what manner of love the Father hath bestowed upon us that we should be called the sons of God" (1 John 3:1). Press on closer into My presence . . . feel the love I have for you. Rest in that love.

There is a seat reserved at My table with your name on it, it has been there since time began. You can get up and leave, but your place is never taken by another . . . it waits for you, it is yours forever. Though you may lose all you have, though you may lose an eye or a fortune, you can never lose your place in My kingdom. No one can ever take your place.

So come, sit, drink, and feast at My table, My child, My precious one. Be filled, be nourished, then go out (yet never without Me), knowing your place in My family is reserved for you and for you alone.

This is real security, this is rest, this is the calm assurance that you really belong, that you are loved, wanted, and needed at home, and that you are as much a part of the family of God as anyone else is . . . yes, as much as Jesus.

Rejoice and learn all that it means to really belong.

Speak Lord

Come into the Holy of Holies now. Worship and praise with thanksgiving is what brings you here every time.

When you come to Me with a pure and repentant heart, washed in the blood of the Savior, your sins are always forgiven and you are free to enter in and experience the glory and the joy everyone can have, yet few have ever really known.

Do not fear to come, I am waiting here for you. I want to take you higher, and you will go higher, daily, if you come to Me as you have done today.

You know the Way: I am the Way. You know the Word: I am the Word. You know the Truth: I am the Truth. You know the Life: I am the Life.

From this day on, the things of this world will grow strangely dim in the light of the glory and grace of the presence of Him Who has opened the way for you.

I will never leave you alone to choose the wrong way. I not only tell you the way to go, I go with you all the way, your hand in Mine. That is the way it will always be, beloved; be secure in this.

Be patient, be at peace, and rest in Me, knowing full well that I am bringing to birth new life in you each day. As you grow, you come closer to the perfection that is found in Christ Jesus.

Be content to let Me work this out in you, to rub and polish until the dull, lifeless areas of My vessel shine with the radiance of My reflected glory. Yes, the rubbing can hurt; it can also be tiring, boring, and you may know feelings of frustration, you may feel unproductive. Yet when the true color bursts forth, you will look back and acknowledge the wisdom of your Lord in how He brought it to pass. So be patient, allow a little more time for a little more rubbing, a little more polishing . . . for the end is not quite yet.

Patience is a quality that is acquired slowly. As the spirit ripens, it grows. Patience can only be gained through experience. You would never become patient if you never had to wait for anything! Leave the timing to Me. Rest and wait . . . I am never too late.

Speak Lord

Behold the table I have spread for you, laden with good things. See how your cup runs over? I invite you now to partake of the blessings I long to pour out upon you. Come and be filled. Your enemies are outside the door . . . they cannot come in . . . ever.

Protection is afforded you today and every day. I walk with you each minute. You are doing My will, and your rewards will come in an eternal dwelling place with Me and Mine. Plant your feet firmly on the path of righteousness and never swerve from the course laid out for you. I will do the rest.

Remember, I am the door, the door to eternal life, eternal peace, eternal joy. You see now as through a glass darkly. Your understanding is so clouded, so limited, that you cannot see what lies ahead.

Imagine yourself sitting in the backyard watching a cat watching a bird with a broken wing. Could you explain the danger to the bird? What must you do? Sometimes you can remove the danger, but sometimes it must be the bird that has to be quickly snatched out of danger. I can no more make you understand My ways than you can make that bird understand your ways. One day, My child, you will understand it all . . . and it will be far more wonderful than your present mind could ever begin to grasp!

Be present at My table . . . My communion table . . . My table of sacrifice . . . My table of banqueting.

You have offered yourself to Me as a living sacrifice; I have received that offering. Now partake of the table of sacrifice, but it is not you who is offered there, but rather it is I, the sacrificial Lamb, offered once and for all to atone for your sins, Who has given Myself for you.

Now there is never any more need to present a sacrifice upon the altar. The one, true, pure, sufficient sacrifice has already been made and that alone is the only acceptable sacrifice for your sin.

"God demonstrates His own love toward us, in that while we were still sinners, Christ died for us" (Romans 5:8). Ponder on the love that prompted that!

Find peace at the foot of the altar of sacrifice. Find rest there, contentment and joy; find the promise and assurance of eternal life.

Drink from the cup of My sorrow and suffering, and it will be unto you joy and health, eat of My body of sacrifice and you receive all of Me, for all I died for has become yours. My sorrow: your joy; My suffering: your health; My rejection: your acceptance. My death: your life.

I invite you now to join Me and feed from the banqueting table of all that is offered there for you.

Be little for Me, for what is small in the eyes of the world is great and mighty in My kingdom.

Fear not to be a fool for Me, for in your so-called foolishness is the wisdom of your God, the all-wise Creator God, Who is the very Author of all wisdom.

"The message of the cross is foolishness to those who are perishing, but to us who are being saved it is the power of God" (1 Cor. 1:18).

Fear not to be ridiculed, for as words of ridicule fall upon your head I form them into a crown.

My crown of thorns has now become My crown of glory and dominion. Now everything the world puts on your head and tries to form into a condemning crown of thorns is the material I take and transform into your crown of glory

"Blessed are ye when men shall revile you and persecute you and say all manner of evil against you falsely for my sake. Rejoice and be exceedingly glad, for so persecuted they the prophets which were before you" (Matt. 5:11–12). Like them, great will be your reward.

Be prepared now for a totally different life. Be open for blessings you never thought you would receive. Because you are a blessing to Me, I make you a blessing to many.

Your lifestyle is about to undergo a radical change. You said I could do surgery on you if necessary. I have been doing that all along, and I will continue to do it until you are perfected in Me.

My surgery need never be painful. If you relax and yield yourself to Me, as you have done, I perform it and you don't even know it has been done!

I have a journey for you to take, and one day soon you will look back on this writing and understand it fully. The path veers sharply now.

The eternal city looms ahead, for your sight is set squarely on the things of the Spirit. My Spirit is pleased with you, and I will manifest Myself through you, for your spirit is right with me and very usable.

Your new life will be a challenge that you will grasp eagerly and be happier than you have ever been before. Fear no changes now, for I have instituted them, and they are with My full approval for you. Respond with unqualified joy, you need have no reservations. This is right . . . this is My will for you. Receive, My beloved, all I have for you.

Speak Lord

Do not fear the unknown. Have I protected you so far only to let you go? Have I nurtured you only to forget you?

You walk daily with Me, seeing Me answer your smallest prayer, yet you waver in faith when it comes to the future. I have held your past, I am holding your present; and I hold your future.

"I know the plans I have for you, plans to prosper you, and to give you a hope and a future" (Jer. 29:11).

Why do you feel abandoned? Remember what I have done for you in the past and trust Me for what I will do for you in the future.

I have told you through the years that you have nothing to fear, yet you allow the devil to steal your joy through apprehension. I call you to do only two things: trust and obey. I will provide everything else for you.

One day, when you stand with Me in the perfected joy and glory of your next phase of existence, your one regret will be all the years you spent in fear and doubt, living so far beneath My will for your life. You allowed the enemy to rob you of joy because of what you thought might happen, which, as you will know by then—never ever did!

Before Abraham was, I AM. Before Adam was, I AM. Before the sun, the moon and the stars, I AM. Before the dawn of creation, I AM. "I AM Who I AM" and that is all you need to know.

Ponder My power, meditate on My might, glory in My grace, and rest in My redemption.

The power of My resurrection, yours through grace, is what I want you to meditate on today. That same power that raised Jesus Christ from the dead now dwells in your mortal body. Ponder this: Behold, I have given you all things necessary for salvation, for victory. So, be at peace; be filled with joy and love.

Look at each day and each person with the heart of Christ, the eyes of Christ, and the mind of Christ. See My lost, hurting ones as I see them. Be My arms to comfort, My voice to give strength, comfort, and love. Be My voice of gentle, yet firm, loving correction. Be filled with My compassion, and, as My anointing remains on you and My power flows through you, you can and will change your world.

So, know with all your heart, Who I am, and, through you, the world can better know Me as I really am.: The great I AM.

Speak Lord

Be ever aware that the righteousness that is yours is imparted righteousness. Yes, you are righteous, spotless before Me, but through nothing that you have done . . . apart from receiving My Son.

You are righteous because you have been redeemed and washed with the precious blood of My Son, Jesus Christ, your Brother, your Savior . . . and your King. Be very aware of this righteousness. "All our righteousness is like filthy rags" (Isa. 64:6). Be also aware that any righteousness of your own, apart from My righteousness, is nothing more than filthy rags in My sight, so it is nothing to feel smug about nor proud to attain.

This righteousness that I see when I look at you was a free gift, to be worn as a priceless robe. Its purity and beauty, beyond anything you could imagine—and you are clothed in this forever—is a love gift from Someone Who paid the highest price ever paid for anything so this robe could be yours. So, beloved, wear your robe with thanksgiving and in humble adoration of the One Who loves you so much that He gave His all for you.

I call you to be consistent in your walk. You cannot be filled with praise until you are empty of self pity. You cannot truly worship until you are empty of pride. You cannot seek Me and seek justification for sin at the same time. You cannot make excuses for the things of the devil and expect to see Me.

Become conscious of the different ways I speak. So many times a great blessing is missed because you are in a hurry and turn blind eyes and deaf ears to Me. Keep the TV set on or you won't get the picture; turn the volume up or you won't hear the sounds. Be careful that you have your dial set at the right channel. If there is interference, clear it as soon as possible or you may miss something important. Stop and be aware of Me. Practice My presence. Talk with Me more; listen more. Turn more to Me and turn more over to Me. Look to Me before each decision. Depend on Me, I will never fail you.

Once you truly seek Me with a clean heart . . . void of the pollution of excuses. Once you truly look for Me . . . not the experience, but just because I am Who I am. Once you seek Me . . . wanting nothing but to fellowship with Me and to bask in My presence. Once you seek Me as you would your next breath, then you will find Me . . . already there . . . waiting for you.

Speak Lord

"Do you not know that you are the temple of God and that the Spirit of God dwells in you?" (1 Cor. 3:16). Always be aware of this.

What does it mean to be a temple of the living God? Sanctification? Yes, and more. A temple is holy ground, and you are right to obey the laws of morality and health so as not to desecrate the temple. God's temple must be pure in every way.

But what else is a temple for? Is it not a place of rest for the weary, comfort for the fearful, and strength for the building up of those who visit it? Is not a temple a place of refuge from the storms of the world? Is it not a place where the hungry come and get fed?

Do those who visit this temple find peace, love, courage, and faith?

A pure temple is necessary so that it can be a pure channel through which My grace can be brought to mankind.

I need an active, growing temple where My Spirit can operate freely.

Purge the temple, yes, but then fill it with food for the hungry, rest for the restless, peace and love so that those who visit My temple will come away refreshed and strengthened.

Be prepared, for greater things, far greater things, are coming your way. All those years that seemed to you to be endless boredom and heavy burdens were but the very detailed preparation for what you are to become. Through these trials you learned patience, longsuffering, forgiveness, self-control, kindness, goodness, faithfulness . . . and most of all you have learned to love.

So give thanks for all that has happened to you in the past. It was the necessary voyage you had to take, but now your ship has pulled into a port of rest . . . not home yet, but you are at a place where you can get out of the stormtossed sea, get your land legs working again . . . rest, relax, and enjoy your surroundings, knowing you are getting closer all the time to home.

Enjoy this stopover now. Sightsee, rest, have fun! Your worries are behind you now, and you are set free. Look forward to all the rest of your life, for it will be a time of enjoyment for you, a time of refreshment, and a time of blessings.

Live in My peace and joy and expect the desires of your heart to be fulfilled, because they will be.

Speak Lord

Because you have rested in Me, I will bless your going out and your coming in. I will fill your emptiness with good things, and I will never turn you away.

You are blessed in My sight, and you stand pure and clean before Me with My robe of righteousness on, worn humbly, but with pride in your Lord.

You proclaim Me proudly, so will I proclaim you proudly to My Father and your Father. "Those who honor Me I will honor" (1 Samuel 2:30). Those who are not ashamed to confess Me do I also confess to My Father and your Father.

Be confident today fear not, for I am with you. Be not afraid, for I am with you, and I am your God. I create . . . and I destroy, I build up . . . and I tear down.

You will know Me better before this day is over, for you will understand in a deeper way how I work in the lives of those who love Me.

Be willing to carry your cross . . . pick it up willingly, and when you do, you will find it is light and easy to bear, for I bear the brunt of it, and it will become for you a joy.

I want to explain now about the narrow way. I did not say the way to Me is hard (I said My burden is light). I did say the way was narrow. Follow straight ahead with your eyes on the goal. Don't go too far either way. Stay on the path. Excess in anything is straying from the narrow path. I am walking ahead of you, all you have to do is follow Me.

My desire for you is that you may have joy in your life. You can have My joy no matter where you are or what you are doing. Once you understand that we can move on.

I have promised you abundance in your daily living, in a world where you will find yourself glad to be alive, joyful and contented in Me.

So, be confident to step forward and grasp what I offer you. Fear nothing, for the only real fear there needs to be is the fear of losing Me, and that is something you need never fear.

So, beloved, believe My promises. I am faithful and I will never fail you. Be keenly aware of Me. I will see to it that you understand My leading. I will not let you down. Be confident, be brave, be open to receive from Me.

Speak Lord

Evangelists can preach to thousands and hundreds can answer the call, but unless even one continues in Me, it is not as valuable as you can be in bringing only one soul to Me, then seeing to it that that soul is fed and nourished. The follow-through, until they are able to walk alone, can be far more important than the initial encounter. Remember the parable of the sower.

Rest in Me and stop being that runaway horse, unbridled and ready to run in any and every direction. Wait for My call, and don't try to outrun or outguess Me. You are still trying to run before you can walk!

Call down the rain of the Spirit upon you and your family. Many blessings are stored up for you. It is time now for you to cash in some of your assets.

There is no law of diminishing returns in the Kingdom of God. The more you withdraw, the more you will have. You cannot drain the reservoir of My blessings.

You have two accounts in the bank of Heaven: one was opened for you the day you got saved. You did not know it then, but at that moment your loving Father opened a joint account in your name and in Mine. At that moment you were made a "joint heir with Jesus" (Rom. 8:17). Do you understand all it means to be a joint heir? Everything you inherit you inherit jointly. Do you realize what it means to you to be a "joint heir with Jesus"?

My wealth is limitless! "The silver is Mine, and the gold is Mine" (Haggai 2:8), and this is a limitless resource. There is no overdraft possible here; the more you withdraw the more your Father deposits into your account!

Like the physical law of use (use it or lose it), you must build your spiritual muscles; the more you use them the bigger and stronger they become.

There will never be a bounced check from this account; it is an endless supply . . . and it is yours.

The other bank account is the one you personally open up for yourself. Your deposits in this personal account will earn far greater interest for you than any earthly bank would allow.

This account is where you plant your seeds, and this is where the law of reciprocity takes over. How much you plant, and what you plant, determines how much, and what, you reap.

Speak Lord

This bank account can remain dormant, and the resources will dry up if you do not deposit regularly. So deposit as much as you can into this account and withdraw as much as you want from the other.

You deposit by your unselfish service to others and by unconditional love. Deposit My life and My word into the lives of others. You deposit by your tithe, by your forgiveness, by being a blessing and a comfort. You deposit by seeing a need and filling it. You deposit when you speak of Me to others and as you live in obedience to Me.

Do these things, beloved, and your rewards will surpass your highest expectations. Watch and see how this personal account of yours will grow!

Your resources in these accounts are overflowing . . . and they only keep on growing!

Count the minutes now before you stand beside Me, when I will impart My glory unto you, when I transform your earthly body of corruption into one of noncorruption.

When I open the locked chambers of your mind and reveal to you all truth, when I take blindness away from you, and you see things no mortal has ever seen—it is then that you will see all the past and all the future, for no more will time be separated into past, present, and future . . . you will see it all as "now." Then, for you, time will be no more.

There will be no more space . . . you will see what is next to you, and you will see into the far reaches of endless space as if they were next to each other. You cannot comprehend this now, but you can dream!

I will take deafness away from you, and you will hear. You will hear the secret things of My Spirit. You will hear beauty in sounds you never knew existed. You will hear the beauty of sounds only heaven can produce.

On that day your understanding will be without limit.

Speak Lord

On that day you will understand the fundamental workings of the universe: all knowledge, all intelligence will be yours. You will see how perfectly everything ties together. (You will never understand healing until you understand everything else.) "For now we see in a mirror, dimly, but then face to face. Now I know in part, but then I shall know even as I am known" (1 Cor. 13:12). With your capacity for joy unleashed, and all that stifled your joy forever gone, you will have an explosion of joy!

What happiness will be yours when all limitations are forever lifted off of you and you become as a joyful child! At first you will even act like a child, flying, leaping, jumping for joy! Singing with the most beautiful voice you have ever heard! Laughing with a mirth you never knew was in you! Dancing with complete abandon! I will stand by and laugh with you, dance with you, yes, and even fly with you. I will delight in your joy!

I want you to flow in what I am doing in this time. Flow in the Spirit and don't be afraid to let the world know it.

It was your confession of Me that sealed your redemption. "Whosoever confesses Me before men, him the Son of Man also will confess before the angels of God. But he who denies Me before men will be denied before the angels of God" (Luke 12:8–9). Do you not see how important your confession of faith is? Never pass up an opportunity to confess Me when the witness of the Spirit is there. Nevertheless, if once you have confessed Me and they receive you not because they have not received Me "then shake the dust off your feet" (Mark 6:11). Let your blessing return to you and leave them, for I would not have you throw your pearls before swine for them to trample upon (Matt. 7:6).

My holiness, My sacredness, is the most precious thing there is, and those who deal with it lightly or flippantly will have a dreadful price to pay for blasphemy against the Holy Spirit of God.

"Walk not in the counsel of the ungodly" (Ps. 1:1). Walk with Me and walk with My children. Walk among the ungodly, yes, but not with them . . . for you are chosen, special . . . a new creation.

Speak Lord

Let your light shine, but if men insist on walking in darkness, then let it be so for them.

Confess Me, walk in the light I have given you, spread the light of My love, but do not defile it. My Spirit will show you how.

Do not run away from all I have for you. Tell My people to come and listen to what I have to say to them, for many are like leaves tossed in the angry wind, "tossed about by every wind of doctrine" (Eph 4:14), not having the knowledge nor the understanding to come and rest in the safe harbor of My love. Tell them that they, too, can hear from Me. Tell them to listen, to spend time with Me.

I call you, not for the lost alone, but also for My children who flounder. I need anchormen. You are to be a stabilizer for those searching, bewildered, questioning children of Mine who lack direction. Your foundation is strong, so have no fear if they lean on you, for when they do, they lean on Me. I have called you to love, not to be responsible for the outcome of it! If people accept you that means they accept Him Who sent you. If they reject you, they reject Me, for I am in you, and you are in Me.

A sabbath rest I have prepared for those who love Me.

Do you know that you can be caught up in a rush of work or activity and yet be resting? The rest you have in Me is not contingent upon circumstances; it goes far beyond that, even as your spirit life goes far beyond the soul life.

Live in this calm where nothing can touch you to disturb your peace, for I am in your spirit, and your spirit is under My control and cannot be touched by outside forces, unless you will it to be so.

I have taken over your spirit, and that same Spirit that raised Jesus Christ from the dead now dwells in your mortal body. Let the knowledge of this sink down into the depth of your soul. Accept this and live like you believe it . . . it is a true and vital life force for you to use for your blessing and for My glory.

I promise you this: I will allow you to walk in what measure you can, for you walk, even now, in eternity. You will be walking in this world with those around you, but your senses . . . your soul and your spirit, will be in a sphere most people don't even know exists . . . and you will be walking in that sphere right there next to them!

I have some Christmas surprises for you! Like any loving parent I delight in happy surprises for My children. I have many happy surprises for you, not only on this Christmas day, but all through the coming year.

Christ was not My final Christmas gift, although in receiving Him you receive the capacity to receive all the others, for all the others are contained in Him. Without you first receiving Him, I can give you nothing.

You have received My gift of My Son, now take the baby Jesus into your arms, hold Him close to your heart, feel His absolute helplessness, realize that this tiny babe can do nothing for Himself . . . His helplessness is complete.

Let the realization sink down into the depth of your soul that this tiny, helpless baby is Almighty God by Whose spoken word the galaxies were breathed! The wonders of this universe (most of which you know nothing) originated with Him.

Realize, if you can, that this almighty Creator and Ruler God chose, of His own free will, to be stripped of all His power and rendered helpless in the form of that tiny child because He wanted to save *you*! He did not have to do this, but He knew the consequences if He did not, and, because of His love for you, He made His choice when He knew full well what was in store for Him.

See that tiny baby . . . grown up now and knowing the choice He had to make that lay ahead for Him. He could have refused the cross and the suffering that no human mind can comprehend; but that was never an option for Him . . . He loved you too much! His was no ordinary suffering and death. "He Who knew no sin, *became* sin for us that we might become the righteousness of God in Him" (2 Cor. 5:21). Ponder this, and respond in love . . . that is all He wants from you.

See that willing Substitute now, as He stands in readiness, awaiting the time when He can come for His beloved Bride. See Him now, in all His glory, with all that He had before restored to Him . . . and more, for He now has His body, the Church . . . His redeemed for whom He did all this.

See Him now, as He is today, and as He will be forever. Ponder on Who He is . . . and Who He is to you. Receive now a deeper insight, a fuller understanding, a greater joy, and a more intense love than you have every had before. This is My Christmas present for you, beloved! This overflowing joy, this inexpressible love is not a gift that you will use up by next Christmas, but an eternal gift that can only grow stronger and deeper as you learn to handle it and dwell in the peace that comes with it.

So take this, My gift for you, with no strings attached. Just receive and enjoy forevermore all that I have given you.

Speak Lord

Lay aside all earthly loads, don't just put them down . . . consciously lay them down on Me; it is My desire to bear them for you.

"Let not your heart be troubled, neither let it be afraid" (John 14:1). I have overcome. I have conquered all. The battle is over forever . . . and you have won! Live that victory now.

When I tell you to claim what is rightfully yours, remember that a part of that is the ability to minister to My people in My Name. You have the legal right, as My heir, to use My name and everything that name implies is yours. In My name is healing, in My name is deliverance, in My name is salvation, in My name is restoration. I give you full authority to use My name, and in that authority you stand with all the power of heaven behind you.

"In My name you shall cast out demons" (Mark 16:17). Marvel not at this, for it is only as you stand in My name, and only in My name, can you do this. Marvel rather that your name is written in the Book of Life, never to be removed. Rest securely in this knowledge, and then take up all this authority that is yours and use it to the glory of your God.

Lay aside all earthly loads, for when you lay them down, I pick them up. I cannot take them from you until you let them go. Release all to Me now... and then rest, knowing you have done all you can.

Then you will know that I have taken the reins and you are not riding a runaway horse, but you will be guided into the deep rain forest of My calm for refreshment, for forgiveness, for restoration, and for renewal.

You will understand my directions, and you will follow them to the letter. I will give you the strength, health, knowledge . . . all you need, to do all I call you to do.

You will know deep peace always, once you have totally mastered this truth. Give it up to Me now: your family, your job, your future, your finances. Trust and rest, and watch Me work it all out.

Always be prepared to serve Me. Keep yourself spiritually attuned, for you never know when you have to offer up a quick prayer and there will be no time to get yourself into "spiritual condition" for answered prayer. Keep your prayer life finely tuned, so that when called upon to pray you will reap the fullest rewards.

Your picture of Me vacillates and becomes distorted. One minute I am the Man from Galilee and the next I am a vision of such magnitude you cannot comprehend Me! I can only be to you what your mind can grasp. Where you are spiritually determines what your view of Me will be.

A baby Christian will see Me as I am portrayed in pictures that men have conceived: "Gentle Jesus, meek and mild." As they grow, their image of Me grows. You will never see Me as I truly am with the eyes of your mind, nor the eyes of your body. You can only see Me with the eyes of your spirit, and that vision is blurred for many reasons.

Perfection is a state never to be obtained on earth. Only after the seed is planted does the tiny seedling emerge. You are still a seed, but you have everything in you to make the perfect tree you will one day be! Don't become impatient with the seed, it can only be so much now, but the potential is there, ready to burst forth.

Your spiritual maturity determines the clarity of the concept. Do not let this discourage you, for you see Me clearer each day, and one day you will stand before Me in My kingdom and you will see Me clearly.

Come into My presence with singing, for there is much for you to sing about.

Healing is being manifested daily in your life, both physical and emotional.

Consider for a moment the past you had and scars that it left. All the hurts, disappointments, frustrations and fears realized could have left you a physical and mental cripple, but I have healed you. There is no longer any area of your life remaining where the past is lurking in the shadows ready to strike and cripple you. I have pierced those dark corners with the searchlight of My cleansing, healing beams of light; the germs festering there have been burned up in the heat of that light. You are whole . . . you are free!

Satan is trying to put fear on you about your future, yet you have My promise . . . and I never fail . . . that you have nothing to fear. No terror by day nor night shall come near your tent (Ps. 91). No famine shall destroy what I have created and recreated in My image. In the midst of desperation, you will walk in quiet places. In the midst of depravation, I supply your every need. In the midst of fear, you will have peace, for I have conquered all.

Speak Lord

For we wrestle not against flesh and blood, but against principalities, powers, the rulers of the darkness of this age, against spiritual hosts of wickedness in the heavenly places. the principalities and powers of outer darkness" (Eph. 6:12). You've learned how to wrestle . . . now you need to learn how to win.

"Put on the full armor of God: the girdle of truth, the breastplate of righteousness, your feet shod with the preparation of the gospel of peace, the shield of faith, the helmet of salvation and the sword of the Spirit, which is the word of God" (Eph. 6:13-17). Now you are protected, washed in the blood of the sacrificial Lamb, and armed with the word of your testimony. Now stand, beloved. Resist the devil and he will flee . . . he has to.

You are part of My end time army. Get in rank . . . the battle is almost over!

I have taken the blinders off your eyes, and now you can see what has been happening to you, and now you know what to do about it. Stand in the victory already won for you, child of the Victor King. The Son has set you free, and you are free indeed.

Grieve not the Holy Spirit Who loves you, Who yearns for your total surrender. Only as you lose all can you gain everything . . . only as you let go can I take absolute control. Stand clad in the whole armor of God:

The Helmet of Salvation . . . know without a shadow of doubt who you are in Me. Do not allow Satan access to your mind. Walk in the knowledge of My salvation and your sanctification. Your mind, covered with this helmet, washed clean in the redeeming blood of the one, true sacrificial Lamb, will be able to withstand the evil the enemy would bring into your life through your thoughts.

The Breastplate of Righteousness . . . *Stand* strong, knowing you are fully armed to withstand any hurt, any blow, any attack of the enemy. My righteousness, My child . . . not your rightness, is all the armor you need to present yourself spotless before our Father; for when He looks upon you He sees Me, for I am in you, and I am covering you.

The Girdle of Truth . . . *Stand* firm in the knowledge and love of God and of His Son, Jesus Christ. The devil is the father of lies, but you are equipped with the armor to discern those lies and to believe and receive only what comes to you from the Word, the Truth, and the Life: your Savior and Redeemer, Jesus Christ your Lord.

Speak Lord

Take up:

The Shield of Faith . . . *and* forever avoid being destroyed by any fiery dart of the devil. The shield of faith is your protection from fear of the unknown, your confidence in the authority that is yours.

Wield:

The Sword of the Spirit . . . My word; use it to cut through all the bondages that have kept you bound. Stand strong in the promises that are rightfully yours and you bring down the foes of darkness, for all the power of Satan cannot stand up against the word of God.

Put on now:

The Shoes of the Gospel of Peace . . . *and* every place you plant your foot will be holy ground. Step out, shod with all you need for walking the walk of the Spirit.

"Peace I leave with you, My peace I give unto you; not as the world gives do I give to you. Let not your heart be troubled, neither let it be afraid" (John 14:27). "And the peace of God which passes all understanding, will guard your hearts and minds through Christ Jesus" (Phil 4: 7).

Now you are fully armed, My little soldier. All you need to do now is stand and remember: The battle is the Lord's.

There is a battle to be waged . . . there is a higher level of spirituality to be reached . . . there are people to be loved and cared for . . . as unto Me.

You do not reach a higher level of spirituality by reading and listening to tapes, those just help teach you and interpret what is happening in you. You reach a higher level of spirituality by truly giving love, for no other motive than because you are being conformed into My image.

Unconditional love is the vitamin your spirit will use to nourish you and grow you up into the fullness of the life I have ordained for you.

There is now no more time for introspective wanderings, for petty things of the flesh. You need now to learn how to live in your glorified body, so that when you get it, you will be far more comfortable with it than with the house of flesh you now think of as your body.

Think on the things of the Spirit, and you will walk in the Spirit and begin to experience a taste of the glories that lie ahead for you.

Think on the things I am going to lay on your heart. Meditate on where you have been and where you are going. Prepare, for you are coming into another phase of your journey upward. Pack your bags and be ready!

Speak Lord

~~~~~~

Deep within your heart there is an unexpressed yearning. You are barely aware consciously that it is there. It plays itself out in longings that lately you barely notice, but they used to be so strong.

You yearned for a place, a special place, beautiful music, dancing for joy, Someone very special to love Who would love you beyond a human's ability to love.

You captured a flash of the realization of these yearnings, sometimes in a bar of music, sometimes in a particular scent . . . it was there . . . just a flash, for a brief moment in time, and then it was gone. The feeling, too intense, too hard to express . . . perfect joy, a feeling of perfect well being, perfect fulfillment, total happiness.

As you grew older and cynicism replaced expectancy, it grew fainter and further away. Now it has all but gone, as the cares of life stifle it and the tears of life drown it out.

Allow Me to recapture for you those moments when you were surprised by joy! Stand still, be quiet now, and allow those flashes a place once again in you. They are but glimpses, beloved, of what is to come!

Allow Me to draw you back to recapture those precious moments. Do you not know what you experienced? Then let Me confirm what you really do know in your spirit: a spirit does not just come into existence at conception. Your spirit . . . like my Spirit, has been in existence from the beginning. Spirits cannot be born, and spirits cannot die.

When those moments come, your spirit is remembering . . . recalling the joyful bliss of your pre-human existence. They call you back to a time before fear, sorrow, pain, disillusion, and distress robbed you of the joy you had in Me, a joy above the capacity of the human flesh to experience.

Now, beloved, the time is drawing closer when you will no longer have only flashes of what is indescribable, but you will live once again in that state for all eternity.

Get excited, for it is all about to happen for you! Fear no more . . . only trust, obey . . . and look forward with speechless expectancy to the joy that is laid up for you in eternity.

Lay down the things of the world, be quiet within and without. Be wholly Mine, be responsive to Me . . . be yielded to Me. Get excited . . . and get ready!

My commission to you now is to love the unlovable. You will not do that well until you learn how; it does not come naturally. The natural man. . . the flesh . . . can only love what appeals to him. The supernatural man (the Spirit filled Christian) has the ability in him to love far beyond the natural.

When you have My Spirit dwelling in you, then you are a supernatural creature . . . born from above . . . now you can do it. Now you can look into the face of that person, now you can think: "Jesus died for you. If His love for you is so great that if you were the only person who ever lived, He still would have come to earth, suffered so horribly, and died, just for you . . . how can I do less than to love you?"

Look through My eyes and you will see another dimension to everything. The eyes of love see much, look above much, underneath much . . . and overlook much. The eyes of love look beyond the surface and see the eternal. Look at all My children . . . the children I gave my life for . . . look on them with the eyes of love . . . look at them with My love.

"This is My commandment that you love one another as I have loved you" (John 15:12). That is a lot of loving, beloved! It is only when you love through Me that this is possible.

I have commissioned you to take My love and the soothing oil of My Spirit to hurting hearts. I have not called you to a chastening ministry! When you chasten, it will be done with such love and tenderness that it will be healing, never adding hurt to hurt.

I have called you to bind up the brokenhearted, to heal the hurting heart, and to set the captive free. I have called you to be My hands extended to a hurting world.

There are those I have called to rebuke with fervor those who walk in sin. I need you to obey your call. Your role is to those in need of strong guidance and the firmness of your rebuke.

For others, the words of Isaiah 61 more nearly apply: "The Spirit of the Lord is upon Me, because He has anointed me to preach the gospel to the poor. He has sent me to heal the brokenhearted, to preach deliverance to the captives and recovery of sight to the blind, to set at liberty those who are oppressed, and to preach the acceptable year of the Lord."

These were My calls when I walked on earth . . . I call you to walk in My footsteps. Love My hurting children . . . love them to life.

Speak Lord

You never need to go through the wilderness more than once if you learn your lesson the first time around. What it took the Israelites forty years to do, you can do this minute.

Learn to obey without grumbling. A test is given you; learn, and pass the test the first time around, and get on with it! Don't linger there, go on now to bigger and better things.

You don't have time to stand over the grave and ponder. That issue is dead . . . let it be dead . . . leave it there with all the side effects buried with it. If you try to dig it up, you will regret it more than you understand. Standing at the grave and looking down you cannot see how rotten is the thing that is buried there and how vile the smell. Leave the grave site and go on.

You won the victory, but Satan is a sore loser. Stand as you are now and don't give in for a moment.

As each thought comes in, cast it out. Do not, for one second, entertain one of these thoughts . . . trust Me with that. I will give you all the help you need.

Remain in victory, stand strong and tall in Me. That victory will be very, very sweet.

Lay aside the grave clothes, for I, the Lord your God, have spoken. I am the authority you turn to, I am the last word in any decision. I am the court of law, the supreme Judge and Justice.

My justice is swift, sure, and merciful . . . thorough, and without change. I don't administer justice . . . I AM Justice.

All the man-made laws ever to have been put into force will have to be weighed on My scale. My gavel is lowered. I am come to bring recompense, and My law is love, compassion, mercy, grace, and justice.

My sentence ends in forgiveness for every repentance, for I see the heart. You can be sure that all who throw themselves upon the mercy of the court will receive a just and merciful sentence if they but lean on the everlasting arms, accept the sentence given in love, by Love, and learn from their mistakes.

All who come to Me will receive total forgiveness. Remember, although I am all justice and My conditions must be met and the law fulfilled; two thousand years ago the fine was paid, the sentence served, the death penalty carried out, and, standing in that great substitution . . . I proclaim you free!

Speak Lord

You are so dramatic! You seek Me in the hurricane but not in the gentle wind. I am in the breakfast and lunch of life, not only the dinner.

The most intimate moments with Me can be spent when you are doing the most unlikely, mundane things.

Great mountaintop experiences can be self-gratifying rather than God-oriented, if all you are looking for is a spiritual high.

When your eyes are on Me, you will find Me in the most unlikely places . . . under the most unlikely situations . . . and you will be truly blessed. Then you will truly know you have been walking with Me, and your heart will sing over the very idea of it!

The peace I have given you is only the first step. I have so much more for you. You are being prepared, don't be impatient. I know how you long for a closer walk with Me, and that is all I need from you. I will do the rest when you are ready.

Suppose I gave you power you couldn't handle? What would you do with it? It would frighten you, and you would not use it, or you would use it indiscriminately (with you it would be the latter). . . and that would be worse! So trust Me, rest in My love, keep close to Me . . . and learn to wait.

Bring to the foot of My cross all I bring to your remembrance.

You are making quite a hill under the cross! I see pride, selfishness, fear, doubt, and self-pity lying in that heap of rubbish. So much is piled there, but there is still so much more to come.

My arms open wide to receive your sorrow and pain, your emptiness, the loneliness that prevails. . . the feelings of being an outsider . . . the hopelessness, helplessness, the inadequacy, the insecurity, the frustration of being and doing where and what you don't like to do and . . . the uncertainties. All this and much, much more.

I loathe what you feel, for it keeps you from Me, and it hurts My child for whom I want perfect fulfillment.

Take a fresh look at what is left in you of the things you need to give Me. You say you have thrown pride on the cross, yet you still care what people think and say about you. Learn to define pride and understand self-respect.

Remember, you are My ambassador: Are you doing this for Me or for yourself? That is what makes the difference. Do *all* for the glory of God. Without Me doing that in you it is impossible, but let Me do all I want to do in you and, as the dross burns away, you will be as shining gold.

If you try to burn the dross away yourself you will burn yourself... and burn yourself out. I know how it must be done. I know what temperature you can take and for how long. So, just let Me do all that needs to be done, just be willing to throw on that filthy heap all the things I lay on your mind as things to be discarded.

I am cleansing My temple—thoroughly, yet gently. With loving fingers I clean and replace the treasures, as well as discard the debris. You will be happy with the finished product!

"Because I live, you shall live also" (John 14:19). Life can only come out of the valley of death. The seed must die to bring forth the sprout. The old self must die before you can be reborn. The process of dying can sometimes be painful. To live every day this way is not easy. Allow Me to crucify you, for you cannot do it yourself. I promise you it will be swift and thorough.

So many things have become second nature to you, things you really enjoy . . . things you don't even think about when you decide to walk in the narrow path that lead to Me. Some things which seemed all right before, now you know are wrong. The Holy Spirit will lead you and show you how to curb your thoughts and retrain your mind. Give Him full rein.

Call all that you have Mine, and all that I have for you will be yours. You are really getting there now, really getting to the place you should be in your journey. You have a closer relationship with Me now; one day it will be perfected, but now it grows stronger each day and will continue to grow stronger as long as you live under the shadow of My wing. "Ask and it will be given to you; seek and you will find" (Matt. 7: 7). You are seeking, you will find.

I don't have any problems, I only have solutions. Give Me your problems, and I give you My solutions. You have taken another step closer to Me . . . another victory . . . another satanic attack defeated!

Rise above all the problems in your life . . . you hold the key . . . you know how it is done. Practice living in the provisions I have for you and reap the benefits, they are all there for you. I don't want you to miss out on one blessing I have for you.

Bring forth all the truth in you and make Me manifest. You have had great teachings throughout your life, most of which were pure truth, some of it was diluted by man's carnal reasoning, but on the whole you have been blessed with much of My truth. You do not see how much a part of you all this has become, yet you live these truths every moment. The thoughts you think, the reactions you have, the motivations . . . all your senses have been affected by My Spirit teaching you through My prophets and teachers.

As I spoke to the prophets of old, so I speak to you today. As I spoke to the prophets of old, so I speak to all My children today who will listen to Me.

Continue to prayerfully seek counsel from the wise, "study to show yourself approved" (2 Tim. 2:15). Learn, and put that teaching into effect in all you do.

Many have fallen by the wayside, and, without the faith and trust in Me to pick themselves up and go on, they lay there feeling condemnation, feeling worthless, feeling helpless and lost. Many there be who have tried to live the Christian life and, not understanding what that means, have fallen under the load of what they have been trying to bear.

There is no such thing as instant sanctification. "Be ye perfect" (Matt. 5:48) means "being made continuously perfected" . . . a growth process.

At the moment of the new birth, a new nature is given you, but there is still much of the old man left, which may take a lifetime to sift away. A lot of the chaff falls through at the first sifting. At the right time the sifting gets finer. I may have to shake vigorously at times to get the chaff to the place where it can be removed. Let this shaking take place. I am removing from you, layer by layer, what needs to be removed.

Do not allow the enemy's condemnation to unsettle you. You know you are not perfect, there are still many areas to be dealt with, but don't try to do it yourself. Submit to Me, and I will work a great and mighty work in you.

I have great things in store for My "getting there perfect child," made in My likeness and redeemed by My blood.

Speak Lord

I have anointed you to be My ointment. Many will come to you, many who are hurting, many whose pains have prevented them from going further with Me.

I have put within you the oil of gladness, the water of the word, the healing balm of Gilead, the power of the name, the wind of the Spirit, to refresh the weary and downtrodden. You are My "watering hole" right where you are, and there the thirsty will find drink. You are My "food kitchen" where the hungry will go to be fed. You are My "oasis in the desert" where the dying will find My life through you.

You need to do nothing but rest in Me, step out in faith and trust Me to do the impossible through you. Do not lean on your own understanding; in all your ways acknowledge Me, and I will bring it to pass.

"The gifts and calling of God are irrevocable" (Romans 11:29). I called you once, I call you again. Come up a step higher now. Trust your spirit to hear from Me. Trust My Spirit to lead, direct, minister, and bear fruit through you. You have not lost the anointing.

"Many are called, but few are chosen" (Matt. 22:14). Because you have answered My call I have chosen you. So now, My chosen vessel, be all I have created you to be.

To give Me every aspect of your life includes your thought life; you will know when your thoughts are from Me and what to do with those that are not.

Satan tried to put thoughts of failure in your mind that would have you give up, he will try to convince you that you are not able. Why would he even bother with you if this were true? His time is too short for him to waste his efforts.

The more tempted you are to give up, the more I say to you: "Receive My mind, My capabilities, My strength, My wisdom, My power, and My anointing." The more you are ready to give, the more you will be supplied. You know your source never runs dry.

Let Me be in you all I want to be, each day at a time. Take no thought for what you shall eat, what you shall wear, or where you shall live, for your Heavenly Father knows you have need of these things.

You will never have a need that I will not be able to supply . . . your ever-present Source . . . Your ever-present Supply . . . Your ever-present Savior.

Speak Lord

My little one, you feel very inadequate now, weak and unable to cope. I say to you, blessed are you, for that leaves no props for you to hang onto, no straws for you to grasp and, unless you continually hang onto the Rock of Ages, you will surely go under. You cannot hang onto your education, money, job, status, or any other aspect of the power structure that the world has built and glorified.

The treasures of the world will be as hay and stubble at your feet on the day of reckoning. You depend on none of these things, so it only remains for you to depend on Me.

So, beloved, come now to the eternal spring. Drink deeply, breathe in My Spirit, feed on Me, let Me dwell richly within you. I desire to take all your inadequacies and replace them with My adequacy, your uselessness and transform it into My effectiveness, to turn your every lack into gain. Where are you the weakest? There is where I will make you the strongest! Those areas where you feel least able to cope, I take and, through My grace—the divine ability to cope—make that very area one where you will be the strongest. Truly in your weakness is My strength, and all your righteousness, which is no more than filthy rags before Me, I will make, as you yield to Me, into the very righteousness of your God.

My people, like a vast multitude of sheep grazing in the field, are vaguely aware that their Shepherd is there and that He will come to their aid when they need Him. Yet many do not have a conscious awareness of My presence. My people . . . a vast multitude, like sheep grazing in the field, so many are unaware of what is happening around them, unaware of the wolf that seeks to destroy them. Leaving that problem to their Shepherd, they only graze upon the food He offers them, and as they feed on the word of God, they become spiritually nurtured, and they grow. Still their Shepherd watches and waits.

One day the Shepherd will say to His flock: "The time has come to move on, for the wolf is ready to attack." The sheep will hear the voice of their Shepherd and they will follow Him . . . not through the valley where tribulation lies, where the wolf waits to devour, but rather He will lead His flock away and out of the reach of the wolf, and the wolf will not be able to touch them.

So, My flock, continue grazing, continue growing . . . with your eye on the Shepherd . . . not on the wolf. Wait for the sound of His voice, wait for His command to move on to greener pastures.

Speak Lord

Lay aside all the encumbrances that weigh so heavily upon you. Walk in the freedom that is your right under the covenant you have with Me.

The last traces of "people-pleasing" bondage and the nagging fears of the future that you have refused entrance are still hanging around outside looking for a chink in your armor. They will leave once they know there is no shadow of a chance that you will ever receive them.

The burdens others lay on you are not meant for you, so lay them on Me and be free. Be free to love them apart from what they do, say, or feel. There is not one too great, nor too far gone, that you cannot effectively minister to them.

Be careful not to let the enemy rob you by giving in to his deception when he tells you that you should turn in another direction because it looks like the going may get tough. That is exactly where the blessings are! Not in escape from the problem, but right in the middle of it all is where you will find the greatest joy, the biggest blessing, the deepest contentment, the most lasting peace, and there, beloved, is where you will find Me.

Go in My strength, not yours, My wisdom, not yours, My love, not yours, My faith, not yours . . . and watch as the Red Sea parts for you!

Lift up your heart in trust . . . lift up your hands in praise . . . lift up your eyes and earnestly seek My face, for I am coming soon. Concentrate on preparing the way.

Would that every person, living and dead, could come with you into My kingdom, but each has been given the will to choose. That is all it would have taken: making the right decision. Many willingly and knowingly did not make the right choice.

Many are there whose will was not developed: the child . . . the retarded, with the mind of a child, or those with no mind. These will be with us, restored to wholeness. It is only those who knew, and willfully rejected, My gift of salvation who will not be there. Out of those left on earth there will be many who will do it the hard way, endure the torture and come . . . wishing they had listened in time. Every possible opportunity will be given to everyone, for "I have no pleasure in the death of the wicked, but that they turn from their ways and live" (Ez. 33:11), but I cannot violate the free will of man. Once the die is cast there is no turning back. "My Spirit will not always strive with man" (Gen. 6:3). "Seek the Lord while He may be found" (Isa. 55:6).

Speak Lord

Make a path through the quiet forest so you may walk with Me as your only companion at certain times in the day. You get busy and caught up in the day's activities, and I am pushed aside until you have time for Me. You are not seeing the forest for the trees!

I want you to enjoy the fellowship of your brothers and sisters, but you are neglecting the very thing that will make that fellowship even more precious and the very thing that will make you grow.

You are like a leaf blowing in the wind! You stop at one place, then get caught up in another gust of wind and off you go again! Where does a leaf belong? It will only wither and die unless it is attached to the tree, where it belongs, where it receives its nourishment . . . its life. As soon as it falls away it begins to die. Keep fast hold onto your Source of life.

You are to feed upon Me through My word, and through personal private communion with Me. These must be your priority every day. See what a difference this will make in your day, see what joy you will have when you do. See how I will hold your hand all throughout the day and nothing will overwhelm you.

Remember these things the next time you are tempted to rush off somewhere before you spend time alone with Me! Make Me your priority and see how much more blessed and peaceful your life will be.

*L*et everything that hath breath praise the Lord" (Psalm 150:6).

Why do I want you to praise Me? Am I some egotistical power Who loves to see His people groveling? Nothing could be further from the truth!

I delight in your praises because of what praising Me does for you:

"Praise binds kings and nobles with fetters of iron" (Ps. 149:8). Not earthly rulers, but the rulers of darkness. Your praising Me reminds Satan of who he is. It weakens him to the degree that he is bound and all his demons with him. When they are bound, you are free to be to be My joy-filled, healthy, energetic, intelligent child, prepared for My kingdom.

Praise also reminds you of who you are: a sinner saved by grace. You cannot be filled with praise and pride at the same time. Praise reminds you that all your righteousness is as filthy rags (Isa. 64:6). . . what you are without Me. Oh, but, beloved, look at who you are *with* Me!

Most importantly, praise reminds you of Who I am.

Speak Lord

*B*lessed are My children who wait upon Me. I promise instant salvation, but I never promised instant healing, instant perfection, instant joy. Many times you need to grow into these things.

I do give My gifts instantly, but when they are not manifested instantly that is when you stand in faith believing you have what you have asked for. "Whatsoever things ye desire, when ye pray believe you have received them, and you will have them" (Mark 11: 24). If you believe you already have what you cannot yet see manifested, then you already have your desire; it only remains to translate the answered prayer from the spiritual realm to the material. That is where it may take time for many reasons.

It may take time to get through Satan's realm (Daniel 10:12–13), and that is where spiritual warfare comes in. It may take time because meanwhile things are being accomplished, whether in you or in someone else, that could not come to pass any other way. It may take time because you may not be ready. It may be that if you knew the outcome of your prayer you would not have asked for it! Your Heavenly Father knows what things you have need of. I will never give you a stone when what you really need is a fish!

My little one, you are My beloved, and I walk beside you. One day you will stretch out your hand, and I will take it and lead you gently into My kingdom . . . and you will never taste of death, but have life eternal.

More, far more than you know, I am with you... I am in you . . . I am around you . . . closer than the air you breathe, nearer than your skin. Breathe, and you breathe Me in. Walk, and I surround you. Sit, and you rest in Me. Lie down, and I overshadow you. Stand, and I raise you up.

As the sound waves are in the air around you, even though you do not see nor hear them until they are channeled into your radio or television, so I need to be channeled into your spirit through prayer.

Draw close, put in the plug, turn on the knob. Make contact, and you will know that I am here. But was I any less there before? "Lo, I am with you always" (Matt. 28: 20). I have promised, I am faithful; yet to reap all the benefits, you must tune in to Me. Turn on the knob by coming apart and communing with Me.

You were "plugged in" at salvation . . . now just turn Me on!

Speak Lord

I will be strength to you . . . I will uphold you. I am ready to pour My Spirit out upon you, and you will be given all the power and strength you need for the tasks and duties ahead.

Let your light so shine that the world will see you as a beacon in its dark night. Follow your light to the Light, the Light that lightens the world: My Son.

A lot of the time you feel like you live in two different worlds . . . as though you are two different people. Come apart and be with Me; I am with you in both worlds!

You feel Me in the love that is manifested in My people when you are with My body. You are at peace, for you sense My Spirit among you. Then it's time to go back into the world, into the unforgiveness, resentment, bitterness, criticism, gossip, and on and on. Your spirit cries out for the communion you have left.

Bring to your remembrance Gethsemane . . . think of Calvary. Do I need to say more?

Take up your cross daily, take it up willingly as I once did, and one day, beloved, one day you will exchange it for your crown!

You have a job to do out there in the darkness. Look around you at the lives I have touched. Look at the faces of My own. The nearer they get to Me the more it shows.

Look at the faces of the lost . . . the longing in their eyes, the haunted hollow faces of those who know nothing of My joy and My life, which I long to impart to them. Look at them, My child: the old, the young, the not so young anymore. A Spirit-filled Christian has the discernment, if they would but cultivate it, to look into the soul of man.

Feed on Me, then feed My flock, and pray that there will be those who will gather up the crumbs under My table.

Make the most of the hour, for the time is short. Let every moment count for Me. Ask: "Is there something I could be doing for Jesus instead of what I am doing?"

Instead of spending time feeling sorry for yourself, spend that time in praise, in thanksgiving, and intercession for those around you. Give thanks in everything, in every situation.

Speak Lord

You talk about serving Me, of going off as a missionary to some far corner of the globe. That is a calling, beloved; you don't just *decide* to go!

The lost are all around you, as lost as any human anywhere could be. Your call is to pray for them.

I have My people strategically placed. You are not where you are through some poorly dealt hand of fortune, you are there by divine decree of Almighty God, to do a job . . . and that job is intercession for those around you.

Be sensitive to My Spirit's leading for if, when, and how to speak to them of Me . . . but always, always, always pray.

Lift up your hands, yea, lift up your heart to the God of all creation: the Almighty Lord of all life: your Father, Who knows how many hairs are even now on your head.

Learn of Me . . . all you can. Rest in Me . . . all you want. Serve Me . . . all you dare. I will use you to the very utmost if that is what you wish. I will give you all you need . . . if you will give Me all you are.

You are called by My Name, that means you are Mine. When a child is born, it is given its father's name because it comes from him and is a part of him and is his responsibility. To bear someone's name means something. Be conscious always that you bear My Name, that you are an heir . . . a joint heir with Jesus, an inheritor of the kingdom, part of a royal priesthood, a child of the King. Act like it!

Let the world know you are special and that they can be too if only they will claim their inheritance. If a benefactor cannot reach the one he wants to be his heir, then that person cannot inherit from him. An inheritor must know that he has received an inheritance before he can begin to spend it. Remember, you are a child of God, an inheritor of the kingdom, a joint heir with Jesus. Understand fully what that means and claim your inheritance.

Lift up your head, you are part of the royal family of heaven. Be not ashamed of who and what you are. There is no higher rank in heaven or on earth than yours! You are redeemed, sanctified, made holy . . . a saint . . . future co-ruler of the universe. What more could anyone want!

Do you sing songs about Me, or do you worship Me in your song? You enter into My courts with praise and into My gates with thanksgiving (Ps. 100:4).

Do you like praise songs because they are pretty and you like to sing them? Or do you sing them because you are reaching out to touch Me?

You sing secular songs because you enjoy singing them; do not sing praise songs for that reason. Of course I want you to take pleasure in singing them, and I want you to enjoy them, but remember, they are *a call to worship.*

Sometimes you can enter into My presence quicker through song than in any other way. So, beloved, remember to Whom you sing, and reach out in your spirit to touch Me as you sing. You will be blessed and delighted to see how easily you can enter into My presence as you truly enter into worship through singing praises to Me. Sing with all your heart as well as your voice. Remember: "The Lord inhabits the praises of His people" (Ps. 22:3). So praise Me in song, beloved . . . be still in your spirit, wait for My presence . . . and then just bask in Me.

You are in the process of becoming ... as are all My children and also those who are not yet Mine and those who never will be Mine ... all are in the process of becoming either more or less like Me with every trial.

Each trial is a test you take, and you are graded on your test just as if you were in school. At this phase of your existence, you are in My school, My training ground for you ... and graduation day is nearly here!

Graduation Day! The day when the sheep and the goats will be forever separated. The day when I will say to one: "Depart from Me, you cursed, into the everlasting fire prepared for the devil and his angels" (Matt. 25:41) and to the other: "Come, you blessed of My Father, inherit the kingdom prepared for you from the foundation of the world" (Matt: 25:34).

For now I give you only a foretaste ... a very small foretaste of the great and glorious things I have in store for you. Your eagerness for this delights Me.

You have no idea of all I have in store for you! How could I even give you a hint? You could not grasp any of it! Yet deep in your spirit you sense it, and this is why you cry out for all you know is to come. It is almost here, My beloved ... I am even at the door!

To order additional copies of

Speak, Lord

Have your credit card ready and call:

1 877 421 READ (7323)

or please visit our web site at
www.pleasantword.com
Also available at: www.amazon.com